A CUP OF CAPPUCCINO FOR THE ENTREPRENEUR'S SPIRIT

A CUP OF CAPPUCCINO FOR THE ENTREPRENEUR'S SPIRIT

AMERICAN INDIAN WOMEN ENTREPRENEURS' EDITION

JERETTA HORN NORD
NICOLE WHEELER
MOLLY TOVAR

Copyright © 2011 by Jeretta Horn Nord,
Entrepreneur Enterprises LLC

ISBN: Hardcover 978-0-9833167-8-7
        Softcover 978-0-9833167-9-4

All rights reserved. No part of this book may be reproduced, or transmitted in any form or by any means, electronic or mechanical, including photocopying, recording, or by any information storage and retrieval system, without permission in writing from the copyright owner.

This book was printed in the United States of America.

Cover Design by Karen Lemley

Additional copies of this book may be ordered online:

www.amazon.com or
www.bn.com

Jeretta Horn Nord
Founder and CEO, Entrepreneur Enterprises LLC
jeretta@acupofcappuccino.com
405-747-0320

CONTENTS

Preface *Molly Tovar* xi

Introduction *Nicole Wheeler* xv

Acknowledgments xix

Chapter One: Local Ideas . . . Global Impact 23

Live Your Best Life   *Karlene Hunter* 25

Find Your Passion   *Lou C. Kerr* 32

It's All Good   *Monica Simeon* 38

Extraordinary Deeds by Ordinary Doers
          LaDonna Harris 44

Dreams Do Come True   *Jo Ann Rackliff-Richmond* 53

Small Steps to Success   *Jeri RedCorn* 58

Chapter Two: Defining Success 65

Dream and Believe, Learn and Achieve
          Freda D. Deskin 67

This Bird Learns to Fly   *Jolene Bird* 73

Serving Native American Mamas and Babies
   Andrea Northcutt Miller 78

Feeding People's Spirits Through Art
   Julie Pearson-Little Thunder 86

Believe In Your Dreams   *Tonya June Rafael* 92

Tiller Research Inc.: History As An Unlikely Business
   Veronica E. Tiller.. 99

Chapter Three: Creativity and Life 105

Strength From Struggle   *Ramona Emerson* 107

Chicks in Charge   *Erin Merryweather* 113

Ohana Artisans—The Hawaiian Girls of the Southwest
   Jan Pruner and Bon Liesener 121

Repair, Reuse, and Recycle   *Eva Hoeft* 128

Native American Women: Know Your Own Value—Value
   Your Own Worth   *Pauline S. Echo-Hawk* 134

Chapter Four: Spiritual Connections 139

Healing Through Heritage
   Rose Twofeathers Hernandez..................... 141

Dance—The Breath of Life   *Rulan Tangen* 149

Connecting Two Cultures—Strength in Sharing
  Sherry Echo Hawk Taluc.......................... 158

Sacred Steps *Tina Sparks* 165

Chapter Five: Connecting with Nature 173

Down to Earth *Deanna Wohlgemuth* 175

Generational Principles: Their Modern Application to
  Business and Personal Success *Lisa Kraft*... 181

The Gift of Clay *Crucita Melchor*............................ 188

Beauty (Care Products) From Ashes
  Laralyn RiverWind 193

Chapter Six: Serving Others 199

Something Substantial to Hold Onto *Kay Oxendine*... 201

Time to be Whole *Karen Yeahquo*.......................... 207

The Power of Sharing Knowledge *Rose W. Robinson* . 213

We Watched and We Learned to "Just Do the Right Thing"
  Ellie and Elvira Hesse.............................. 220

Hope Nation *Stephanie Kettler*................................ 226

Chapter Seven: Living the Dream 233

Mother & Mentor   *Nicole Wheeler* 235

Believe and You Will Achieve   *Bobbie Nell Vigil* 240

Videography with a Vision   *Rhonda LeValdo-Gayton* ... 246

A Positive Partnership   *Maggie George* 253

Indian Oprah: On My Own Terms
     Margo Gray-Proctor 259

Bibliography 267

Submit Your Story 269

*To all American Indian Women Entrepreneurs
and Aspiring Entrepreneurs*

Preface

Stories at a mother's knee . . . stories to rekindle memories of loved ones . . . stories told by elders at Pow Wows . . . stories evoking memories of the Native past . . . stories handed down from mothers to daughters. It is the *story* that gives a culture and people sustainability. It is through the *story* that we gain wisdom and knowledge, as our curiosity is piqued by the word pictures presented to instruct and teach.

Storytelling allows people a chance to get to know one another. Through the story, cultural values are often introduced, especially to the next generation. Cherokee storyteller Freeman Owle claims that storytelling is a "two-way interaction," giving the listener a chance to offer input and form an identity. The story offers a person that sense of belonging—of knowing who you are and where you came from.

It is the *story* that gave us a sense of our past and a guided path to the future. The stories of three special Native American women, LaDonna Harris, Wilma Mankiller, and Helen Maynor Scheirbeck, inspired us on our life journey. LaDonna Harris, a member of the Comanche Nation of Oklahoma and Founder of Americans for Indian Opportunity, is an activist in civil and women's rights, economic opportunity, and environmental protection. Her personal story revolves around "Indian 101"—sharing the history of Native Americans in order to show the importance of cultural identity, tradition, and values.

Through her experiences as a tribal advocate worldwide, she offers a unique perspective—both as a woman and as a Native—to complex social problems. Her philosophy, a set of core indigenous values, became known as the Four R's—Relationships, Responsibility, Reciprocity, and Redistribution.

Wilma Mankiller, former Principal Chief of the Cherokee Nation of Oklahoma, served as a role model for developing strong women in leadership roles. Her story of accomplishment revitalized the Cherokee people and demonstrated to Native women that they can be respected and accepted as leaders. Her philosophy simply stated: *People learn to survive by helping each other.*

Serving as Senior Advisor for Museum Programs and Scholarly Research at the Smithsonian Institute's National Museum of the American Indian, Dr. Helen Maynor Scheirbeck recognized the power of the story to influence education. Used traditionally by Native communities to pass knowledge on to succeeding generations, the story—among other forms of learning—could serve to inform teaching models used by educators everywhere; Dr. Scheirbeck's vision has been set in motion through the National Education Initiative at the Smithsonian.

The stories of those who have gone before have taught us that, to be "great" in anything you do, you must connect with your family, friends, colleagues, and even customers, to learn—and learn from their stories. Through these connections, you will be able to draw on their spiritual, emotional, and physical knowledge and resources. Your most valuable currency is relationships and emotional capital. While conventional measures of business success can't—and shouldn't—be ignored, human connectivity is the next frontier with which to create growth and a two way interaction.

American Indian and Alaska Native women entrepreneurs have a story to tell. Many of these successful women talk, not only about their accomplishments, but also about adversities and challenges they face. They often share, from an indigenous perspective, ways for women to move toward empowerment in the business world and success on their own terms, utilizing and enhancing their cultural values.

Stories passed on create an intimacy, a bond between the teller and the listener. Many of these stories began as one-on-one conversations as women began sharing their narratives, often unconvinced that they had done anything worth talking about. But important lessons on self-determination, education, networking, and the relentless pursuit of a dream have emerged to inspire and encourage a new generation of Native entrepreneurs.

Stories will be known only as long as they are told. If they cease to be told, part of that cultural knowledge will be gone forever. *A Cup of Cappuccino for the Entrepreneur's Spirit* seeks, therefore, through indigenous storytelling, to preserve the rich history of Native women entrepreneurs and recognize their ongoing success; it is also our hope that these stories will help form an intimate bond of identity with women of all cultures.

Molly Tovar

The terms American Indian, Indian, Native American, Native, Native Hawaiian and Indigenous are used interchangeably throughout the book, depending on the authors' usage.

Introduction

American Indian women are and have been at the forefront of community and national development, however this story is largely untold.

Native women have always been entrepreneurs. Turquoise jewelry is one example of this rich history. Unearthed by Indigenous peoples in the Americas around 200 BC, this mineral, beloved for its beauty, was used for adornment, ceremony and commerce. The Aztecs and Anasazi used turquoise pre-contact, but more contemporary American Indian tribes were able to leverage it as a resource during the 16th Century. The Navajos of modern day Arizona, New Mexico, Colorado and Utah were primarily responsible for teaching other southwestern tribes how to craft jewelry. They realized that accessories were a status symbol in Spanish society and used this knowledge to learn new skills and profit from their products. Over hundreds of years, the Navajo learned not only how to make jewelry, but also how to negotiate and trade with the Spaniards. Archeologists have found beads in Spanish jewelry dating back to this period that indeed indicate social status. Artists Jolene Bird and Tonya June Rafael, featured in this book, are still capitalizing on this tradition and tell their stories of how their craft was handed down from generation to generation.

A Cup of Cappuccino for the Entrepreneur's Spirit: American Indian Women Entrepreneurs' Edition, honors the tradition of women leading communities. These are true stories of women utilizing entrepreneurship to create jobs, goods, and services while building community wealth and strengthening the economy. This book utilizes the indigenous concepts of storytelling and knowledge redistribution to capture and share the accounts of all levels of respected entrepreneurs.

Traditionally, women in American Indian societies were respected because of their role as Bearers of Life, but this comes with the responsibility to ensure that a sustainable environment exists for generations to come. For centuries, and long before the word entrepreneur was introduced, women were leaders in their communities, mastering skills, networking and negotiating to ensure sustainability. Elaborate trade routes wove throughout the Americas. Women were a large part of what would be considered today a multinational economy. Post 19th century anthropological accounts have often been told by Anglo men, who did not understand the complex societal structures and silenced the women's stories.

Today, we are experiencing a renaissance of American Indian women enterprises. A 2004 survey by the Center for Women's Business Research found that 90,000 privately held companies are owned by American Indian women, 1 out of 11 American Indian women are business owners, and American Indian women have the highest rate of entrepreneurship among major ethnic groups. According to the U.S. Census Bureau, the number of American Indian-owned and operated businesses in the mid-nineties doubled, and in 2002 the National Commission of Economic Development suggested that this trend is continuing. Our mission is to ensure that this time not only are these stories told, but that the stories also educate and inspire others to positively impact their communities.

Although popularized in the last decade, social entrepreneurship has long been inherent in the business models of American Indian commerce. Typically working on behalf of their communities not just themselves, women used their cultural knowledge to create their own businesses. These skills often were not defined or even talked about, because they never needed to be. They were implicitly taught from one generation to the next, a modern day succession plan. Helen Cordero, whose innovation brought her instant acclaim and too many commissions to complete in her lifetime, and Louisa Keyser a woman considered the greatest basket maker of all time both revived vanishing art forms and remained steadfast in their traditional practices despite high demand for their work. In the early part of the 20th century, Tonita Pena broke ground painting works that depicted women in their traditional societal Pueblo roles. Each used traditional knowledge to unselfishly bring resources to her community, enlisting others, teaching, and being ambassadors for her tribe.

An acute understanding of community and cultural values has enabled American Indian women to succeed for generations. All of the entrepreneurs in this book emphasized the need to act in a way that is right or good and told a story illustrating their worldview. Many of the women indicate the concept that one should never have to dig deep to recall your business purpose because it drives every day decision making based on values and integrity. It is what helps Native people survive and become successful in their own definition. The current economic climate has had a profound impact on American Indian communities. Currently, approximately 24% of Native women live in poverty and in states like Montana and South Dakota, the figure is above 40%. Fortunately, families are embracing entrepreneurship to find creative solutions to address the economic crisis. Stories in this book illustrate how women have decreased unemployment and poverty, increased personal and tribal financial assets, and fostered the development of human capital for their children and community.

Submissions for this book ranged from stories of emerging entrepreneurs to well established business owners and even to entrepreneurs making a global impact. Each story is a personal narrative recounting how the woman decided to embark upon her endeavors, what inspires her and how she turned her ideas into reality. The essays explore diverse definitions of entrepreneurship and indigenous empowerment that are pushing women toward different thinking around economic and social change. There are examples of American Indian entrepreneurs asserting self-determination, encouraging community involvement, supporting education and economic development, and empowering aspiring entrepreneurs. *A Cup of Cappuccino for the Entrepreneur's Spirit: American Indian Women Entrepreneurs' Edition* recognizes the rich history and continued success of Native women. We hope you join us in celebrating the accomplishments and the future of American Indian women.

Nicole Wheeler

Acknowledgements

Sincere appreciation is extended to the following:

Molly Tovar and Nicole Wheeler for traveling the country to capture engaging stories of American Indian Women Entrepreneurs. These stories are *real* heart felt stories that will inspire, educate and empower others for years to come. Thank you Molly and Nicole for celebrating the lives of these amazing women by capturing, writing and publishing their stories.

The American Indian Women Entrepreneurs who are included in this book for realizing the importance of helping others through your stories. Congratulations on your successes and accomplishments.

Daryl Nord, my husband, for supporting my dreams and giving me energy.

Nicholas Nord, our son, for always being a ray of sunshine and my biggest fan.

Jason, Jenny, Zachary, Rebecca, Audrey and Patrick. You are loved and appreciated!

My family and friends. Life would not be the same without you.

To Molly, Nicole and the women whose stories are published in this book for giving me a deeper understanding and appreciation of the American Indian culture.

Jeretta Horn Nord

We would not have been able to write this book without the extraordinary assistance we received from various individuals like, Carol Schuermann, each of the American Indian women who permitted us to tell their stories in such depth and several friends and colleagues.

Carol, our editor, always had her office door open as she guided us through the follow up process, contacted the entrepreneurs to set up meetings and provided them with the documents necessary to print their stories. It was essential to the integrity of this project that supplemental information on the women we were interviewing was collected. Carol played that role as well.

The women entrepreneurs included in this book had businesses to run, families to take care of and events to attend. We are thankful for the time they took at the end of their busy days, on weekends and evenings to tell us their stories.

The friends and colleagues who encouraged us and supported the idea of this project made a difference in our persevering and crossing the finish line.

Jeretta Horn Nord invited us in the summer of 2009 to assist with her vision of creating a series of books, *A Cup of Cappuccino for the Entrepreneur's Spirit*. Her vision is to make a difference in people's lives and the economy by inspiring, educating and empowering entrepreneurs and aspiring entrepreneurs through success stories which tell not only of entrepreneurs' successes but also of their adversities and challenges. When Jeretta and I met for the first time, I didn't realize the wonderful opportunities this project would provide in traveling the nation to interview Native women entrepreneurs and the vast amount of knowledge that was captured and is now being shared with others through this book. Jeretta provided support through her experience and made sure all the pieces found their way into print.

We would like to thank Lou Kerr, for recommending us for this assignment. It was during a difficult time in our lives, and this project gave us a purpose. Mrs. Lou Kerr, President of the Kerr Foundation and one of the founders of the Fellows Program has been a role model for many indigenous women across the world. She continues to mentor women from all fields, disciplines and cultures. Lou has helped us to make connections and encouraged us to build upon our talents and to believe in ourselves. Freda Deskin, founder of the ASTEC Charter School provided positive words during the process when encouragement was welcomed.

The featured entrepreneurs are intelligent women with passion, perseverance, integrity and a strong work ethic. Through this book, we hope to raise an awareness of their products and services and to inspire, educate and empower others.

Molly Tovar and Nicole Wheeler

Chapter One

Local Ideas . . . Global Impact

In business, you have to always be open to new opportunities.

—*Karlene Hunter*

Live Your Best Life

Karlene Hunter—To "Be Tanka" means to live your best life: in harmony with your spirit and with the earth. Tanka products were created to help you do just that. I am an Oglala Lakota on the Pine Ridge Reservation, South Dakota, with a deep commitment to helping the People, the Buffalo and Mother Earth.

I was born in Denver and spent the first 18 years of my life between Colorado and South Dakota going to school through 12th grade in Denver and spending summers at my grandmothers in South Dakota. After meeting my future husband in South Dakota, I permanently relocated to the Pine Ridge Reservation.

As a wife and mother of three daughters, I worked full time and went to college at Oglala Lakota College completing an Associates in Social Science, a Bachelors in Human Services and an MBA. As I was completing my master's degree in business, I became more aware of the economy of the reservation and realized that the dollar left the reservation within 48 hours. In order to change the economics of our reservation we had to change and turn over the dollar at least seven times. Our daughters were young and I wanted to be on the forefront of changing the economy of the reservation so in 1996 I quit my job at the college and started a business, Lakota Express—Direct Marketing Company, in the basement of my house.

Lakota Express, Inc. (LEX) is a full service management/direct marketing company with a state of the art Customer Service Call Center. This is a true blended service center environment featuring inbound and outbound telemarketing, data entry, order processing, e-marketing consumer service, product or information fulfillment, quality control, survey, and lead generation. Our goal is to customize our service to fit the needs of the business whether it is to take care of customer communications, process orders, coordinate a conference, develop a fundraising campaign, or manage a donor or database.

After four years, we moved to an incubator in Kyle, SD and built a 6000 square ft. facility. Tribal members make up the staff of full-time and part-time employees.

In 2006, I co-founded a second venture, Native American Natural Foods. Native American Natural Foods, LLC, is focused on creating a family of nationally branded food products that are delicious and that promote a Native American way of wellness that feeds mind, body, and spirit.

Beginning with its first product line, which features Tanka Bar, Tanka Bites, Tanka Dogs and Tanka Wild, we provided a category of natural healthy choices in a marketplace that did not exist. I am blessed to be a part of an authentic business that produces quality products and services. Our products are made from buffalo meat and cranberries, have no preservatives and are gluten free. By adding value to traditional Native food products, using modern scientific methods and the least amount of processing possible, Native American Natural Foods innovates value-added products for the U.S. consumer marketplace.

With 44% of our Native population having diabetes and an average life expectancy of 56 years, we have got to get our people back to eating healthy.

The world we imagine embraces the lifestyle that Native American people lived just over a century ago. "Tanka" is used in reference to delivering your best with all your heart, mind, body and spirit. It is the choices that you make and the actions that you take to be who you are. Whether you're Native, white, black, yellow or brown, it is your ability to overcome, to extend a helping hand for those in need, to defeat racism, to protect our Mother Earth, and to love all others on our planet.

Although we now have our products in over 4,000 retail stores in 50 states, this success has not come without challenges. Entrepreneurs on reservations face uphill battles. The tribal land is governed by the Bureau of Indian Affairs. Lease terms are for five years and banks do not like to loan money based on a five year lease. Infrastructures have to be put into place including road systems and technology. Weather and the distance we must travel to buy groceries also presents challenges. The fact that 20 years ago there were only two private businesses on the reservation and now there are 200 illustrate the determination, stamina and perseverance of our entrepreneurs.

Despite the growth of private enterprises, there is still a 70% unemployment rate due to the lack of jobs. It has been this way for the past 100 years. Only within the last two generations, have our people had an opportunity for secondary education. Poverty issues are huge. We have 55,000 enrolled tribal members with an average per capita income of $5600 per year. We have to face these issues, line them up, and knock them down.

I want better for our community. Whatever sacrifices we have to make to better our community, that is who we are.

Key success factors for me have included having a survival mindset, passion, partnering with others, Native to Native—buying and selling, and dedication to people who are helping you accomplish what you are doing. I also depend heavily on technology. Being from one of the most isolated areas in the United States, technology levels the playing field. We have been using social media as a marketing tool for years. Our staff is very social media savvy. That has kept us alive. We have people dedicated just to social media and interact with over 40,000 individuals. Through social media, we educate people on health, our tribe and drive them to our website.

I actually consider myself a social entrepreneur—creating jobs, helping start a chamber of commerce on the reservation and mentoring others. We have a double bottom line, it isn't just the dollars. The nation recognizes this—we give back in so many ways and encourage others to do the same.

First and foremost, however, is being a mother. This affects my children, my grandchildren, and my community. That's what I love about being an entrepreneur. We are making a difference in our world.

My advice to aspiring entrepreneurs is to love what you are doing—if it is not your passion, you will not succeed. You will spend many hours working in your business. If you don't love it, you are not going to stick with it. If you love what you are doing, then it is not work. And . . . in business, you have to always be open to new opportunities.

Karlene Hunter

TRIBE: Oglala Sioux

SOCIAL MEDIA: FACEBOOK: Tanka Bar TWITTER: Tanka Bar

BEBO: Tanka Bar MY SPACE: Tanka Bar

WEBSITES: www.tankabar.com; www.nativeamericannaturalfoods.com; www.lakotaexpress.com

EDITOR'S NOTES: Karlene Hunter is CEO and co-founder of Native American Natural Foods, a multi-million dollar company based on the Pine Ridge Reservation in South Dakota. She is also the founder and CEO of Lakota Express, a direct marketing firm. Karlene serves on the Board of Directors of the National Center for American Indian Enterprise Development. She has also served on the Board of Directors for the Native American Rights Fund; the National Indian Business Association; and the Pine Ridge Area Chamber of Commerce. Ms. Hunter, who holds an MBA from Oglala Lakota College, has received numerous awards, including the 2007 SBA Minority Business Person of the Year for South Dakota.

Find your passion. Ordinary women can be extraordinary entrepreneurs through education and commitment!

—*Lou C. Kerr*

Find Your Passion

Lou C. Kerr—"I want to do and be everything," was my response when adults asked me what I wanted to be when I grew up. That little girl's wide-eyed dreams have evolved into a lifetime spent trying to make a difference. I have spent much of my life committed to creating additional opportunities for women in an effort to aid in their advancement in business and leadership. My goal is to help women be the best they can be through education and mentoring.

I grew up as one of ten children and learned to be innovative so I could earn my own money. At seven years of age, I picked up golf balls that were left behind, cleaned them with bleach, and resold them to golfers. Later, I worked as a floral designer, waitress, and bookkeeper. In high school, I loved economics because we conducted experiments in the stock market. After graduating from high school, I worked in a photography shop before accepting a job as a receptionist for KWTV.

In 1969, I began my first real entrepreneurial venture after convincing a banker to loan me $25,000 so I could open an exclusive dress shop, The Jade Boutique. In 1972, I made a decision to sell the shop. During this same year, I married my husband Robert S. Kerr, Jr., and stayed a busy housewife while taking up golf and tennis. I also traveled a lot and helped with political campaigns.

In 1982, I became involved at The Kerr Foundation, Inc., a philanthropic organization that provides funding to charitable causes both locally and nationally. In 1986, four new Kerr Foundations were formed and my husband, Robert, and I became the President and Secretary of the current Kerr Foundation. Today, I serve as President and Chair of this foundation, which has given more than $25 million to charities and projects including arts and media, medical, agriculture, and historic preservation.

I have always been extremely involved in organizations, activities, boards, and philanthropic endeavors. In 1992, I formed a partnership between the Oklahoma Chapter of the International Women's Forum (IWF) and Oklahoma State University to host the annual Women's Business Leadership Conference. Women leaders from across the nation who have experienced personal and professional success speak each year to an ever increasing number of women. The IWF is an organization of pre-eminent women of significant and diverse achievements who help prepare future generations of women leaders. The Oklahoma IWF accomplishes similar goals with a strong local network. I also work to further enhance the status of women as an appointee to the Oklahoma Commission on the Status of Women and as a member of the Women's Leadership Board at the Kennedy School of Government at Harvard University and the advisory board of the Women Presidents' Organization.

To promote the rich traditions of American Indian arts and culture, I founded Red Earth, Inc. in 1983. The museum hosts a respected collection of more than fourteen hundred items of Native American fine art, pottery, basketry, textiles, and beadwork. Both traveling and permanent exhibits are featured.

My philosophy is that entrepreneurs must commit to giving back to the community from the time they first start their business. Money is not the only way to give back. You can join an advisory board, become a mentor, or volunteer your time. You can never give too much. As long as you are involved, whatever you are able to give—your time, expertise, or financial commitment—you are helping others and will be intrinsically rewarded.

I continue to look to new opportunities and issues that will enable me to expand my knowledge base and personal experience while continuing to give back unselfishly to what I believe in most: people and the community. Find *your* passion. Ordinary women can be extraordinary entrepreneurs through education and commitment!

Lou C. Kerr

TRIBE: Cherokee

WEBSITES: www.thekerrfoundation.org, www.iwforum.org

SOCIAL MEDIA: FACEBOOK: Lou C. Kerr

EDITOR'S NOTES: Lou C. Kerr serves as President and Chair of The Kerr Foundation, Inc. and is Founder and Chair of the Oklahoma International Women's Forum. She has committed her time, expertise, and funds to numerous organizations. Lou currently sits on the board of directors for multiple organizations including the International Women's Forum, Lyric Theatre, Committee for a Responsible Budget, the Women's Leadership Board of the John F. Kennedy School of Government at Harvard University, Women Presidents Organization (Co-Founder) and others.

Kerr chaired the Oklahoma Centennial Commission, the State Capitol Preservation Commission for almost two decades, and continues to serve on the Oklahoma Status of Women Commission. Lou was appointed by President Clinton to the 1995 President's Oklahoma City Scholarship Fund Advisory Board, which funded scholarships for children who lost parents or were severely disabled as a result of the Oklahoma City bombing.

Among numerous awards from the International Women's Forum, Lou Kerr has won the "Women Who Make a Difference" and the "Leading Lights" awards. Lou received the Inaugural "Woman of Valor" Award from *travelgirl* magazine. Kerr was a NAPA Honorary Fellow and was inducted into the Philanthropy World Hall of Fame. She is listed in the Oklahoma Women's Almanac, and was named one of eighteen of Oklahoma's Most Influential Women in 2001 by *Oklahoma Family* magazine. Oklahoma Governor Henry issued a proclamation naming March 2, 2005 as "Lou C. Kerr Day."

Lou enjoys tennis and traveling and is admired and respected by many. Lou C. Kerr is truly an extraordinary entrepreneur!

Lou C. Kerr's story originally titled "The Extraordinary Entrepreneur" is reprinted from *A Cup of Cappuccino for the Entrepreneur's Spirit Women Entrepreneurs' Edition I.*

For every negative there is a positive. For every mistake there is a solution. When we believe and practice this......it's all good.

—*Monica Simeon*

It's All Good

Monica Simeon—A few years back my company was growing by leaps and bounds. The pace was so hectic that I was falling down trying to keep up. I gained customers but I lost a few as well on this bumpy road.

Last week I paid a visit to a customer I had lost. I guess I could have whined about growing pains, apologized profusely and relied on a spreadsheet that showed how much money I could save them if they gave me another chance. To be honest, that was my game plan.

I arrived early for the meeting. I was prepared and ready to go. After their team members were seated, I began my presentation. Seated at a distance was a team member who was disengaged. She wasn't listening to me. She was leafing through the handouts and spreadsheets I provided. It became apparent that she was the person who was most disgruntled.

I know this person. I have been in her shoes at various times in my life. When someone caused me problems, I would get angry. If those who wronged me tried to make amends, I would often become skeptical and mistrusting. There were times my mind was made up before I even gave myself a chance to listen. All of us have been stubborn to a fault at one point or another.

I efficiently went through the presentation and explained how my company increased capacity, reduced prices, and improved distribution. I was quick, clear, and concise. In business, we tend to think things should be cut and dry. Sometimes we think life should run the same way, but that's far from the truth.

On this journey as an entrepreneur, I have learned life lessons that speak to the very core of my existence. One of those lessons unfolded last week at this meeting. The time came when I asked those at the table for their comments. There were the usual "thanks for your time" and "you addressed all our concerns" comments. Then the disgruntled team member had her say. She was quiet at first and slow to begin telling me exactly how my company failed her. But soon every sordid detail was laid before me.

It would have been instinctive to become defensive. However, rather than make mental counterpoints to her criticisms, I shifted my thinking and just listened intently. I took full responsibility in my mind for her complaints. I am not going to say hearing the truth is an easy process. I believe we can block ourselves from acknowledging the things about us that need improving. When we listen with an open mind we facilitate a positive opportunity for resolution and improvement.

At the conclusion of the meeting, I witnessed the softening of animosity. The first process of moving past a bad experience is to take an active step to create an environment where change is possible. When we exercise our ability to listen honestly, we can address our shortcomings. Many of us have faced this challenge throughout our lives but have refused to take that first step.

Growing pains are tough in business and in life. The point of growth is to expand and improve. If, during the "aches and pains" of personal growth, we become so overwhelmed with disappointment, stress, and anxiety, we will sabotage our transition to harmony and balance.

I would say the best result of growth is the opportunity to reflect and take responsibility for the mistakes of the past. It's surprising how many of us actually don't take a hard look at how we contributed to a problem. It is way easier to blame others for the whole mess rather than take ownership and seek partnership for resolution.

I am not sure if I will win the customer back. But when I left that meeting, I felt empowered. I transformed a tense business encounter into a positive situation where I could grow as both an entrepreneur and a person. How we become stronger, healthier and happier from growth is up to us. Anxiety is often our first reaction to conflict and problems. Each of us has the power to flip that into patience and compassion as we listen intently and take responsibility. For every negative there is a positive. For every mistake there is a solution. When we believe and practice this . . . it's all good.

Monica Simeon

TRIBE: Spokane

SOCIAL MEDIA: FACEBOOK: Sister Sky; TWITTER: 1sistersky

WEBSITE: www.sistersky.com

EDITOR'S NOTES: Monica Simeon is CEO and Principal Partner of Sister Sky. In 1999, Monica and her sister, Marina Turningrobe, launched the Sister Sky line of bath and body products at a retail kiosk in Franklin Park Mall, Spokane, Washington and now have expanded the company into a multi-million dollar business by building a fully automated manufacturing facility on tribal land focusing on wholesale distribution. Sister Sky's mission is to create natural products inspired by herbal wisdom of Native American culture. Native Americans have rich and meaningful plant traditions respecting nature's own healing herbs from the Earth. Honoring these traditions, they formulate their products with a guiding principle: Infuse botanical ingredients to enhance health and wellness. Sister Sky products share Native American herbal wisdom to a worldwide audience in an authentic and respectful manner that promotes harmony, balance, education, sustainability and cultural sharing.

Sister Sky has been featured in FORTUNE Small Business magazine and on CNN/Money website. They were recently awarded the Tribal Business of the Year Award by the American Indian Business Leaders Association. Monica believes that positive social change and economic empowerment of Native communities is possible through business ownership. She and her sister are committed to serving as positive role models in Native American communities promoting entrepreneurship, socially responsible business development and sustainability through economic diversification.

In some small way, perhaps those first tears which flowed in the place of words have become the universal language that gave a clear voice for justice for the unspoken needs of Native people.

—*LaDonna Harris*

Extraordinary Deeds by Ordinary Doers

LaDonna Harris—My work in advocacy began in the 1960's. I had no literature, no pre-conceived plans, certainly no proven model of success for how to help Native people. All I had was a full heart and tears of frustration when nobody seemed to understand the painful history and current plight of Native Americans.

My family background partially prepared me for my fight against discrimination and work toward positive race relations. Raised by grandparents of mixed cultures, I watched and learned as they respected each other's differences. However, outside my home, while I could not pinpoint discrimination at that young age, I sensed it as the dominant culture worked to "assimilate" me. For example, my Comanche language was only used at home, for my traditional schooling required that I learn English. Fortunately, my marriage to Fred Harris resulted in a positive blending and respecting of cultures.

Being an Oklahoma State Senator's wife opened doors for me to serve and advocate for Native Americans. The Southwest Center for Human Relations Studies at the University of Oklahoma called on me to participate in a seminar on black/white relations and labor/management relations. This I did, but being somewhat naive to the workings of politicians and professors, I innocently asked about consideration for Native Americans. I was shocked to learn that the Center had little awareness of Native problems and did not even recognize or acknowledge issues of such great concern to American Indians. As I began the first of many crash courses on Indian history—Indian 101—my realization of this covert racism and frustration at my own inarticulation came to a climax as I burst into tears. Ironically, while my feeble words could not adequately explain, my heartfelt tears said it all.

From that moment on, I unknowingly became a political force for justice.

Our grass roots movement for change began in my living room in Lawton, Oklahoma. The Southwest Center was founded with the mission of extending the resources of the university to Southwest communities faced with civic conflict and controversy. Together we looked for ways for American Indians to be part of the local civil rights agenda. Here is where my knowledge and background (Indian 101) became important to our approach. What most people did not realize is that federal policy for people of color, especially African Americans, was to *integrate* into the dominant culture, that is, to be united with and become an integral part of the culture, gaining equal opportunities. For American Indians, however, the policy has always been *assimilation*—not unification but conformity, adjustment, and absorption into the white culture. For nearly a century the Department of Interior had been dictating the lives of American Indians, controlling their unique education, health, and economic concerns and thereby contributing to discrimination and low self-esteem. Our approach was determined by our philosophy and our world view that culture was a strength and should be reaffirmed, not removed. We began to focus on bringing this covert bias to light within the schools, working to create awareness and acknowledgement of the value of cultural retention. Our priority for change was to reduce the dropout rate of American Indian students in Oklahoma, which, in certain districts, currently sat at an astonishing 75%. It is often more difficult to change policies than simply create new ones, so our group worked with high schools to develop pride and self-confidence through Indian Clubs. These clubs offered incentives for participation, including attending a state-wide meeting where keynote speakers such as Sargent Shriver, Fritz Mondale, and Bobby Kennedy encouraged and supported their efforts.

Progress was slow and not without resistance, but eventually we were able to build a successful network that positively impacted the community, and from this Oklahomans for Indian Opportunity (OIO) was born. OIO became Oklahoma's first state-wide American Indian organization. Soon after, I was approached by Iola Hayden, a fellow Comanche with a Master's degree in Social Work, who wanted to participate in these meetings. Her insightful ideas and intellect made her a natural for the position of director. Our staff members were mostly generalists, not specialists in economics or healthcare. So we again had to teach our knowledge of Indian history, culture, and policy to gain the attention of others who could catalyze change. We saw a need and tried to fill it.

At this same time, my town of Lawton was still racially segregated. Like so many towns in this era, the railroad tracks divided the blacks from the rest of us (American Indians were on the "white" side of town). Now many of us in Lawton saw another need—discrimination of African Americans. So my living room became the center of yet another grass roots movement, integration. We observed firsthand how our young black innocents were denied access to movie theatres and how it pained those who fought for our country to be refused service in restaurants. So each Thursday friends, neighbors, clergy, and various concerned individuals met to work for change. We quietly influenced restaurants, banks, and stores one-by-one to open their doors to people of color. Not only that, but we worked to procure jobs and decent employment for African Americans as well.

OIO's approach was simply to raise the awareness of an issue. Our experience helping integrate Lawton taught us that American Indians were not even on the radar of most people. The city of Lawton was established after land occupied by the Kiowa, Comanche, and Apache tribes was opened for homestead in 1901. The city has always had an American Indian presence, but this call for integration did not include American Indians. There were vocal opponents to the integration of African Americans, but the complete neglect of the American Indian population once again unveiled a covert racism. Those who worked for change in Lawton did so without confrontation, but because many individuals made personal decisions to affect change, a powerful critical mass emerged. The violence that erupted in many southern cities during the Civil Rights movement taught us that confrontation often just hardens people's positions.

I attribute our success to Comanche culture. Iola and I personalized the issues by filtering them through our Comanche values and used those values to guide our plan of action. Our methodology was simply trial and error. When things didn't work out we didn't fault ourselves—we just changed our strategy. Once we were able to raise awareness and involve more people, they could help address the issue and take it to the next level.

We never talked about failure; instead, from our perspective the timing just wasn't right. We believed that if you listen to all perspectives—even opponents—collaboration can create a plan that benefits everyone. We were not looking for personal or organizational success, but community progress. When we did succeed, to us this reaffirmed that our cultural approach was valuable. American Indian values humanize an issue while most western approaches require a winner and a loser. This win-loss worldview can kill the spirit. When we did face an obstacle, instead of declaring ourselves losers, we would study barriers, identify the people in charge on all sides and how we influence one another, and work to create a new dynamic where everybody could win.

In that period of unrest that was the '60's, my husband was elected to the United States Senate. Shortly before, in 1964, President Lyndon B. Johnson announced his War on Poverty, and Congress passed the Economic Opportunity Act, which formed the Office of Economic Opportunity. The Office of Economic Opportunity initiated and oversaw programs such as Job Corps and Head Start. Oklahoma tribes were not part of the state's plan when awarding money, so OIO helped change the policy to make Oklahoma tribal governments eligible. As Sargent Shriver's volunteer assistant, I worked to secure funding to fight the Department of Interior's "colonial policy", which controlled resources on Indian lands. OIO worked to raise tribal poverty to a national consciousness. I even testified before Congress (the first Senator's wife to do so) for continued funding of the War on Poverty.

A number of the programs started through the Office of Economic Opportunity proved to be beneficial to Native Americans in particular. Head Start, for example, proved to be a confidence builder for Indian children. In the mid-70's, when the program was about to be terminated, several heads of Indian tribes spoke out and advocated for Head Start. Because of the active support of these Indian leaders, not only was the program saved for Native Americans, but it was reinstated for all children. The impact of the War on Poverty, and the Office of Economic Opportunity in particular, is still evident in tribal communities today, and Native Americans are considered one of the main beneficiaries of the initiative. Not only did it ensure tribal control and self-sufficiency, but it empowered Native Americans to rise to leadership positions within their tribes, communities, and states.

In a collaboration involving both national and local Indian organizations, Americans for Indian Opportunity (AIO), a national organization in Washington D.C., was formed, with a nationwide Board of Directors. It was here that I was again confronted with the fact that many public decision-makers had very little understanding of the issues they were advocating, thus becoming a barrier to effecting change. Back to Indian 101! AIO began educating federal departments and members of Congress to the fact that tribes are governments with certain autonomies recognized by the U.S. Our goal was—and still is forty years later—to interpret current policies in light of the American Indian culture, as well as advocate for social and economic policy changes. We networked and built relationships with other national organizations such as the Urban League and Common Cause. Learning their methods helped us, and they, in turn, incorporated some of our American Indian values into their approach.

Forty years ago there were but few national American Indian organizations. Today, because of individuals who did no more than see a need and provide a space, there are thousands working to advance the rights of indigenous peoples. Our causes have evolved over the years, but our overall mission has stayed the same. We seek to maintain our cultural identity while living and working in a contemporary world, and we strive to raise up leaders who will incorporate our cultural values as they work for social and economic change for indigenous peoples worldwide.

In some small way, perhaps those first tears which flowed in the place of words have become the universal language that gave a clear voice for justice for the unspoken needs of Native people.

LaDonna Harris

TRIBE: Comanche

EDITOR'S NOTES: Ms. Harris has received numerous awards for her work, including "Outstanding Indian of the Year (1965)", a Lifetime Achievement Award from the Institute for Indian Art, and recognition on the cover of the March/April 2011 edition of *Native Peoples* magazine. She is proud to have her family as advisers—including ex-husband, Fred. Her oldest daughter, Kathryn, is an adviser to programs on discrimination, and younger daughter, Laura, is director of AIO. Among her many accomplishments was her successful advocacy for the return of the sacred Taos Blue Lake to the Taos Pueblo in New Mexico.

Always keep in mind "This is my dream." No one else has the vision, motivation, or dedication to make it come true.

—Jo Ann Rackliff-Richmond

Dreams Do Come True

Jo Ann Rackliff-Richmond—I became interested in the art of pottery making in 2002. What started out as a hobby soon became a passion. I took pottery lessons from Larry Thompson, an adjunct instructor at Northeastern State University and an artist. I first saw his work at an art show and appreciated his talent, so I wanted to learn from him. After about four months of lessons and practicing on my own, I began to branch out and develop my own style of pottery making. Whenever I could, I would take lessons to improve my skills and knowledge. Anna Mitchell, an elder master potter, taught me how to use the paddle to shape and size, how to use a slip of different colored clay to put color on the pots and how to burnish to get a better finish. A person is considered a master potter because he or she has been a potter for over twenty years, gained recognition and won awards, and taught others the art of pottery. Jackson Narcomey, a Creek painter whom I met at an art show, continued to encourage me and pushed me to enter contests and participate in shows. This helped me gain confidence and network with other artists. I entered art shows and won awards at museums across the Southeastern United States. With my pottery and baskets I have gone to shows in Alabama, North Carolina, Illinois, Arkansas, Tennessee and Oklahoma. The shows are juried, which means your art must be approved as quality art by a board before you will be invited to participate. I plan to attend the Native American Art Show in Santa Fe, New Mexico, next year. Santa Fe is known as one of the biggest Native American Art markets in the United States.

Originally, my sisters and I began this venture together. It was somewhat comforting to have the support and encouragement of each other, and there was the feeling of "safety in numbers." However, we disagreed about the direction we wanted to go with our business. We decided that it was best to go our separate ways. Striking out on my own was frightening, and it would have been safer to quit. But I was determined to move forward. My efforts were rewarded when I was invited to a pottery gathering in Alabama. This event was over five days and included as many as thirty artists. Southeast potters from all over the United States met to demonstrate and attend workshops on history and the significance of pottery from the 1700's to the present. Seeing this much talent in one place and being considered on the same artistic level was overwhelming! It was then (2004) that I realized my own worth as an artist, and I realized that, yes, I could turn my passion into a successful business!

Even though I had some success in this business, I felt a need to continue to learn as an artist and to incorporate more of my own culture into my work. I went to more workshops and learned about the cultural aspects of pottery. Here I was exposed to museums that housed pottery dug from actual ancient mounds. The beauty of those time-honored pieces inspired me to work harder to promote the Cherokee culture in each piece I designed. I had the privilege of learning from Patsy Hanvey and Tammy Bean, Southeastern Potters, who replicate pottery for museums.

My pottery is traditional Cherokee pottery, that is, it is hand formed, incised or paddled, and pit-fired after the ways of the early Cherokees. For each pot, I dig the red clay myself. The wood smoke burns into each pot, giving it an aged look. Because it is all handmade, no one piece can be duplicated exactly—every piece is distinct and unique. After examining my pottery, one archeologist, Dr. Kelly at the Cahokia Mounds Museum, Collinsville, Illinois, proclaimed that it was the closest he had seen to pottery dug from the mounds—high praise!

Because of my perseverance and willingness to keep learning, I have been rewarded through my business, and I have been honored to show my work at the Smithsonian in Washington D.C., as well as the American Indian Society Inaugural Ball and Pow Wow.

It is a brave person who, in spite of obstacles, continues to pursue her dreams. Nothing is easy that is worth doing, so my advice to those who are just getting started is to continue to persevere. Keep learning and growing as a person. Have an idea, think it through, and work toward that goal. Take time to learn—be patient. Difficulties will come, but with time comes knowledge and wisdom. Always keep in mind "This is my dream." No one else has the vision, motivation, or dedication to make it come true.

Jo Ann Rackliff-Richmond

TRIBE: Cherokee

EDITOR'S NOTES: Jo Ann is one-half Cherokee and she has been married to her husband, Dusty, for thirty-eight years. He supports her in her endeavors but takes a "hands off" approach as far as the running of the business is concerned. They have a daughter and son, three granddaughters and another baby on the way. Jo Ann says that so far none of them show very much interest in art, but they are still young. She has aunts, uncles and cousins who are master craftsmen in Cherokee art.

Through Jo Ann's accomplishments, she has been recognized as an award winning potter and basket weaver. Jo Ann has been invited to the Native American Art Show at the Cahokia Museum in Collinsville, IL as the "featured artist". She was also one of the featured artists in the Native American Women Artists of Oklahoma "Voices in the Tall Grass" art show at the Pioneer Women's Museum in Bartlesville, Oklahoma in 2005.

Networking at art shows builds her clientele and gives her a chance to meet collectors and buyers from all over the U. S. and even overseas. Curators from museums and art show coordinators look for artists to invite to their own art shows. These shows are a major part of her success.

Live every day the best way you can, and try for your dream. Don't fault yourself if you must start again because you are trying something new and you are always learning.

—Jeri RedCorn

Small Steps to Success

Jeri RedCorn—When I first started my company, I wanted to make it part of my soul. The idea developed in me more like a simmering rather than a full boil. The more I thought about my business, the more excited I became, but I took little steps to get where I am today. I knew I wanted to retrace my Caddo ancestry to help me understand what pottery making was about and all of its meaning. Through many different experiences, I learned the history of the Caddo Tribe which helps me create my pottery and put my soul into the creations.

Ancestors of the Caddo Indians were residents of the Piney Woods, thousands of years before initial European contact with the Caddo in the mid-1500s. Successful agricultural techniques and vast trade networks were in place long before the French and Spanish arrived on the scene. Caddo pottery was made for practical purposes, such as cooking pots or storage vessels, which was able to withstand fire. This coarser pottery was often quite plain and undecorated as opposed to the Caddo fine pottery. Caddo pottery fine wares were made thinner than the coarse wares, decorated and polished. Fine Caddo pottery was smooth and covered in various geometric designs. The finer pottery also served to fulfill ceremonial needs. Clay deposits, common in the lands of the Caddo, mixed with water and temper were used to create Caddo pottery. Caddo potters, usually women, used the coil method to create their pottery and then fired it in an open fire. Although I was greatly influenced, I was driven to capture my dream only later in my life, years after my teaching career.

I worked as a math teacher in 1966 at Riverside Indian School in Oklahoma. I didn't have an interest in making pottery at that time, but I knew teaching in a classroom would not be my lifelong work. I thought, then, that there had to be other subjects to teach and in different ways. Later, when I was a stay-at-home mom, I started making my husband's dance clothes. I made ribbon shirts, belts, and the many pieces needed for a man's straight dance clothes. These clothes are more formal than everyday clothing.

My interest in Native arts was picqued when a friend of mine, Supreme Court Justice Yvonne Kauger, invited me and others to a lunch meeting to discuss an idea she had about American Indian cultures. She knew that there were Native people who had great skills, knowledge, and contributions to make in the creating of what is now called Red Earth, a festival featuring Native American visual and performing arts. She wisely gathered around her those individuals with similar values and vision. She tapped the potential of those individuals and utilized local resources to reach her goals.

One such individual was Allie Reynolds, who became the first Chairman of the Board of the Red Earth Festival. Allie was a natural choice because of his prestige, honor, and recognition by the public. Allie was a professional baseball player with the Cleveland Indians and the first American League pitcher to pitch two no-hitters in the same year. He was the recipient of the Jim Thorpe Lifetime Achievement Award for his many accomplishments. So it was natural that Allie would want a traditional Stick Ball game at Red Earth. I was then chosen as Executive Director for Red Earth and spent much of my time tenaciously promoting this new undertaking and soliciting funds. At that time, many people had not seen a Pow Wow, and even the Board and Chamber of Commerce members, while they promoted Indian art and artists, knew very little about Pow-Wows, alligator wrestling, stickball, and traditional crafts. It was not easy—this concept was so new—but we were able to raise over $250,000. This success empowered me and helped me realize my own potential. The seed to start my own business was planted.

During this time I was not making pottery, but I was working with the Caddo people and was introduced to Caddo pottery in Idabel, Oklahoma. Dr. Jim Corbin of the Red River Museum demonstrated coiling pottery and showed how he fired it. That was my total lesson—one. But it was here that the spark in my soul was ignited; I knew then that I needed to be a cheerleader to keep the pottery tradition alive. I took what I learned in that one lesson by Dr. Corbin and continued to experiment on my own. Meanwhile, the planted seed of owning my own business was developing roots. Now I had a product!

In the meantime, in 1987, Red Earth became a reality. One of the first things I noticed was that there were potters from the Southwest, but there was only one potter from Oklahoma, Anna Mitchell. It was then that I realized I needed to participate and show the world that Oklahoma tribes are potters.

One of the challenges I faced was selling my work. I did not have a place to sell and no community support systems that could help promote this type of work, like the Pueblo people have in New Mexico. Another big challenge was getting people to buy my work because the Caddo pottery looked so different than work they had ever seen before, so I had to rethink my strategy. I then knew I needed to become an advocate for teaching people about Caddo history and art. I was able to draw on my knowledge of education and teaching for this task. Then I got a break! I was invited to the Smithsonian to be a consultant to a show called "Born of Clay." I was able to select two of my own pieces for show and was privileged to help select other pieces from the Smithsonian permanent collection to show. In addition, the Smithsonian National Museum of the American Indian purchased three of my pieces for their permanent collection.

This was an experience I will never forget. The reason I had been selected was because of my experience as an Artist in Residence at the Chicago Art Institute in 2004. During my time at the Institute a book was written called *Hero, Hawk, and Open Hand, (2004).* It was very detailed information about the Mississippian Indians and pottery including Caddo. In the book a story was written about my experiences in reviving Caddo pottery, accompanied by a photo of one of my pieces.

One accomplishment that I am particularly proud of is that I was able to convince other Caddo artists to form a Caddo Artist Co-op and enter Red Earth. Five of us entered together, marketing our products as a group. It makes good business sense to support one another. All of these experiences have helped my business blossom and grow.

If I had to give advice to anyone about pursuing their dreams, I would say live every day the best way you can, and try for your dream. Don't fault yourself if you must start again because you are trying something new and you are always learning.

Jeri RedCorn

TRIBE: Caddo

SOCIAL MEDIA: FACEBOOK: jereldine.redcorn

EDITOR'S NOTES: Born of a Caddo father and a Potawatomi mother, Jeri Redcorn was raised in Colony, Oklahoma, on her grandmother Francis Elliot's Caddo land allotment. The quest for higher education took her to Plainview, Texas, where she earned a BS from Wayland University and then to State College, Pennsylvania, for her MA from Penn State. She married, raised a family, taught school, worked in an early Oklahoma Indian Headstart program, served on the Caddo Tribal Council, and was the founding director of Oklahoma's annual Red Earth Festival. Jeri taught high school geometry in Oklahoma City for many years before her recent retirement and today lives with husband Charles RedCorn (Osage) in Norman, Oklahoma.

Having learned how to make Caddo pottery, one of Jeri's most important goals is to pass on the knowledge she has gained to other Caddo women, especially younger women.

Jeri appreciates the closeness to the earth of women who dug clay to make the pots that became her passion. A self taught potter, she uses the techniques of her ancestors. Since she is reclaiming this lost art, she imagines what their tools were. She hand coils, burnishes, engraves and wood fires her pots. Jeri's pottery has been exhibited at the Smithsonian's National Museum of the American Indian, Smithsonian's George Gustav Heye Center in New York and Art Institute of Chicago.

Her piece "Intertwining Scrolls" was chosen by the Obamas to be permanently on display in the Oval Office at the White House. Jeri visited the White House in 2008 as a Rockefeller Fellow of Chicago's Newberry Library.

Chapter Two

Defining Success

To be successful, it is important to believe in and trust yourself.

—Freda D. Deskin

Dream and Believe, Learn and Achieve

Freda D. Deskin—Dream and Believe, Learn and Achieve is written across the home page of The Advanced Science and Technology Education Charter Schools' (ASTEC) website. That simple philosophy sums up the way I have lived my life. These same words have also provided the inspiration for countless learners to discover that regardless of background or ability, they can reach their highest potential and experience a meaningful life while practicing personal accountability.

I was born in Pasadena, California, and spent time in Arizona and California before moving from Hollywood, California, to a farm in Lexington, Oklahoma. I had just finished seventh grade and, as you can imagine, this move provided quite a change in scenery and lifestyle. When my dad bought chickens, cows, and pigs, I initially was intrigued by the novelty of the animals and I gave each one a name. Quickly I learned I didn't want to drink cows' milk and I was afraid of the chickens.

Dad was always an entrepreneur. He invented a piece of equipment for the Bureau of Reclamation to help clean canals. Mother, one of eleven children, understood the value of hard work. My parents instilled a strong work ethic always demonstrating problem solving, discipline and responsibility.

I had a fabulous teacher in sixth grade, Mr. Phillip Wilson, who made a difference in the lives of his students. Mr.

Wilson's influence made me want to someday make a difference in the lives of those younger than me.

After marrying my high school sweetheart, Bob, we moved to Edmond, Oklahoma. Less than one year after we were married, Bob was sent to Vietnam and was MIA for several weeks. These were difficult times, but he returned and we were married for thirty-one years.

Knowing that education was important to my success, I obtained an elementary education degree with a minor in physical education, math and English from the University of Central Oklahoma. I went on to earn an M.A. in secondary education and a Ph.D. in curriculum and instruction from the University of Oklahoma. I was also fortunate to study at Harvard University in the Strategic Management program.

In 1978, I started a program in Oklahoma called "Odyssey of the Mind," an international program that teaches and rewards creative problem solving for students in kindergarten through college. Team members apply their creativity to solve problems that range from building mechanical devices to presenting their own interpretation of literary classics. They bring their solutions to competition on the local, state, and world levels. Thousands of teams throughout the U.S. and from about twenty-five other countries participate in the program. Over thirty years later, this program is still thriving.

In 1985, I was selected as a finalist in NASA's "Teacher in Space Project," becoming one of only one hundred individuals in the world with the official title of "U.S. Space Ambassador." The Teacher in Space Project began as a NASA program announced by President Ronald Reagan in 1984. The goal was to inspire students, honor teachers, and create interest in mathematics, science, and space exploration. Over eleven thousand teachers applied for the program and I was fortunate to be among the final twenty. This was an exciting time for the entire nation that ended in the worst nightmare possible when Christa McAuliffe and six other astronauts died in the Space Shuttle *Challenger* disaster in 1986.

The shock and sorrow of this event served as motivation to inspire and educate children in science and space exploration in other ways. In 1986, under my leadership, Oklahoma's first aerospace summer camps were launched. More than twenty years later, the program has grown to include tens of thousands of participants including outreach programs and teacher training throughout the United States. NASA and the Challenger Center continue to work closely, providing materials and ongoing trainings for the Space Ambassadors. I was fortunate to have served in the capacities of Curriculum Developer, Advisor, Consultant and National Faculty Member to the Challenger Center for Space Science Education.

As an educator, I taught for fifteen years at the pre-collegiate level and nine years at the university level. I served for six years as a university dean before founding ASTEC in 2000. This was Oklahoma's first "startup" charter school and my answer to better prepare youth for responsible citizenship and success in the work force of tomorrow. Today, nearly one thousand students are enrolled in ASTEC.

My latest endeavor has included study to earn an advanced level certificate as a consultant from the American Feng Shui Institute. This inspired the launch of my most recent company New Day Feng Shui with products to balance the energies of any given space to assure the health and good fortune for people inhabiting it.

To be successful, it is important to believe in and trust yourself. The late Oklahoma Chief Justice, Alma Wilson, served as my mentor and taught me how to trust myself and how to negotiate personally and professionally for a "win-win." It is also important to give back. We teach this to our students by supporting a number of non-profit groups. Because I "Dream and Believe, Learn and Achieve," I have been blessed with great success.

Freda D. Deskin

TRIBE: Cherokee

SOCIAL MEDIA: FACEBOOK: Freda Jones Deskin

WEBSITES: www.asteccharterschools.com, www.newdayfengshui.com

EDITOR'S NOTES: Dr. Freda Deskin has been honored with many awards including "Woman of the Year" for Oklahoma by the Girl Scouts and the Newcomer of the Year award from the Last Frontier Council of the Boy Scouts. She is a two time honoree of "*The Journal Record's* Fifty Women Making a Difference" in Oklahoma. She received the Frank G. Brewer Award for the Southwest Region from the U.S. Air Force for outstanding contributions in aerospace education and the prestigious "By-liner" award by Women in Communication. Freda was named the Outstanding National Educator from Women in Aviation in 2007. She also received the Marita Hynes Award for Excellence from the University of Oklahoma for her lifelong encouragement of women and girls in sports. Because of her work with curriculum development and Microsoft's Flight Simulator, Dr. Deskin was invited to a small dinner party and dined with Bill Gates in his office. Freda has one son named Sam and two toy schnauzers named Alma and Wilson.

Freda D. Deskin's story "Dream and Believe, Learn and Achieve" is reprinted from *A Cup of Cappuccino for the Entrepreneur's Spirit Women Entrepreneurs' Edition I*.

When times are slow or you feel discouraged, just keep going, keep trying. With hard work, you will eventually be able to "take off."

—Jolene Bird

This Bird Learns to Fly

Jolene Bird—I am now ready to leave because you are taught very well. These were the last words I heard at the bedside of my dying grandfather. He has been gone now 15 years, and yet his teachings live on in me every day. He gave me the tools I needed to be successful. Of course he motivated me and taught me to succeed in the business world, but more importantly, he worked with me and helped me gain the confidence I needed in any life situation.

I spent my young years in the security of my grandparents' home, watching and learning. Both of my grandparents were skilled in jewelry making. My grandmother did beading and my grandfather worked with rough turquoise and a variety of shells. I spent most of my time with my grandfather, who taught me how to slice the turquoise and shells, shaping them, then grinding, sanding, polishing, and drilling holes until they were ready to be strung. I would go with him when he went from store to store, meeting with buyers and negotiating business deals. Upon finishing high school, I took accounting classes at the local community college and then spent six months at the University of Las Vegas continuing my education. Even though my education wasn't completed, I know now that it formed a strong background for my future as an entrepreneur.

When I was 20 years old, my grandfather encouraged me to become more involved with the making and selling of jewelry. He always told me, "You will do well." At this time I was making mostly necklaces and earrings. But Grandfather had more in mind for me. I think it was his plan to take this young Bird and teach her to fly! He began grooming me for the business. Under his watchful eye, I was now expected to go from store to store and actually do all the negotiating while he waited outside. At first I was embarrassed, shy and scared to be facing those buyers who were used to dealing with my experienced, respected grandfather. But I never questioned his decisions or motives. Over time, I, too, began to develop relationships with store owners and eventually was recognized as a skilled business person in my own right.

My grandfather's matter-of-fact expectations and encouragement gave me the confidence to continue even when I was frightened. His determination to push me out of the nest was never more evident than in my twentieth year. One day, he declared that this was the day that I was to buy a truck. Vehemently, I protested—I didn't have a job. How could I possibly afford a truck? How would I make the payments? His reply was non-negotiable: "Get up early every morning and work hard." He had provided me with strong motivation to succeed!

Wisely, Grandfather taught me economics. Early on, he showed me how to reinvest in materials for my business, and he taught me to budget and save my earnings. I worked closely with him for three years, and gradually over the next 6 or 7 years, he let me assume more responsibility. It took almost ten years for me to learn all aspects of the business. The entire venture was a family endeavor, both of us sharing the expenses and profits. After that third year of working closely with my grandfather, I began to turn some profit, and I was allowed to keep the money. I was now flying solo. What began as participation in small craft shows close to home in New Mexico expanded to larger shows in an ever widening geographic circle, including Arizona and California, and eventually from coast to coast.

I *was* taught well, but not just in the jewelry business. My grandfather taught me how to live my life. He taught me how to raise my children. He taught me how to work hard, have confidence, and take care of my family—including my grandmother after he was gone.

I continue to hone my craft. I spent about four years learning new skills to be able to enhance my necklaces. What started as traditional jewelry making has evolved into more contemporary pieces, and I have added bracelets and even silver purses.

I have been in business now for twenty-eight years. I love being an entrepreneur because I love traveling and meeting new people all across the country. But what I love best about being an independent business owner is that nobody tells me when I have to get up!

My best advice to those who are "testing their wings" in the business world is to have patience. It may take years and you have to start at the bottom. When times are slow or you feel discouraged, just keep going, keep trying. With hard work, you will eventually be able to "take off."

Jolene Bird

TRIBE: Santo Domingo

EDITOR'S NOTES: Jolene continues to sell jewelry, preferring to do so at Indian Markets, face-to-face with her customers. She is invited to shows based on the craftsmanship and style of her work, in addition to her reputation. Jolene mentored her mother who now has her own jewelry space in Santa Fe. Jolene currently lives in Santo Domingo Pueblo, New Mexico and has two children, Claudine and Charles, and one grandson, Verdel Zane Bird. In her spare time she loves to travel with her family and play with her grandson. She also enjoys running and shopping.

If you have a vision and follow your heart, do not give up on your dream. If you want something badly enough, keep at it until it works. Your purpose in life will be revealed to you if you look for it, but you need "eyes to see and ears to hear" – once you find it, work at it with all of your heart . . . as if you are working for God!

—*Andrea Northcutt Miller*

Serving Native American Mamas and Babies

Andrea Northcutt Miller—It was a difficult career ladder I had to climb for 25 years, as an Executive Assistant to high-level professionals, but I always knew the jobs I had were not what I wanted to do with my life. When I was a young girl, my parents knew I was interested in working within the Native American communities, but they let me design my own path and find my own way. It wasn't until I grew older and wiser that my interests in midwifery and trusting birth powerfully emerged.

Midwives and doulas are recognized as responsible and accountable professionals who work in partnership with a pregnant woman to give the necessary support, care, and advice during this time; this relationship continues through the labor and the postpartum period, helping during birth, supporting breastfeeding, and providing care for the newborn. This care also includes preventative measures such as education regarding proper diet, exercise, and even emotional and spiritual wellness. In this service, I am tasked in health counseling and education, not only for the woman, but also within the family and community. I gained my training by apprenticeship with a Certified Professional Midwife, continuing education through Ancient Art Midwifery Institute and membership of the Childbirth and Postpartum Professional Association (CAPPA). I believe that the services of midwifery and birth/postpartum doula are ongoing learning experiences.

My business has been built mostly by word of mouth or through doula websites. I usually begin with a mama in early pregnancy and stay with her, officially, through postpartum; but so far, I have stayed in touch with many of these women ever since. Many families send pictures of the baby when he or she is one year old and often continue to stay in touch beyond that first year. Usually, appointments are once per month into the second trimester and then every other week to every week depending on the need. I try to teach them about the importance of a good prenatal diet and exercise to build strength and stamina for labor – it's hard work! I teach them about the importance of a sound mind during pregnancy, talking to the baby with love and reassurance. We talk about preparing for breastfeeding as well as encouragement and education about such issues as soreness, engorgement, and mastitis; we prepare for labor and I share knowledge of possible complications and what to do in case of unexpected issues; and finally, I educate the mother regarding the postpartum period which includes the possibility of depression and how to recognize it, bonding with the baby and sharing with the daddy, and taking care of herself during this time.

My job is not complete just because a baby arrives. As every mother knows, that is when a woman needs the most help! I continue to provide services to women, sometimes for weeks after the birth of the child, such as breastfeeding support and consultation, as well as light cooking, light cleaning, and even running errands. Through this long-term care, close relationships develop; we gain intimate knowledge of one another, and a special bond of trust is formed.

The general public often has the mistaken idea that midwives are, on one end, either not "qualified" care professionals or are "birth saviors" – neither is true. The word midwife means "with woman." A midwife is someone who serves a mother, baby, and family during pregnancy, birth, and postpartum. A midwife is a server, not a savior. People may hesitate to use a midwife because of fear of birth, lack of trust in their ability to birth naturally in their own environment, or because of peer pressure—*"Everyone goes to the hospital to have a baby."* This affects my service because our western culture is fear-based when it comes to birth. However, once a woman has had a natural birth experience in her own environment, her eyes are open to the way God designed birth. She is ecstatic, euphoric, and overjoyed with the event of childbirth. An example of a response comes from a mama I served saying, "Her calming presence gave me the strength to focus on what was important. I was able to overcome those moments of doubt because of her warm compassion."

I strive to help women maintain a healthy pregnancy and a natural birth experience. I am trained to recognize and deal with deviations from the normal ways of women giving birth by obtaining certain skills and knowledge. A vision I have is to strive to understand the Traditional Native American beliefs regarding birthing and childbirth. Because of this, culturally competent health care is important to know, since each tribe is different and has its own customs.

I want to accommodate tribal beliefs by learning through relationships with Native midwives and families.

Most Native women on and off reservations now follow the traditional western medicine. However, there are still some birth customs that set Natives apart. The one thing that is normal for Native births (that may or may not be true in western culture) is that every family member in the county will show up for the event. The entire pregnancy is exciting for everyone in the family and community. Thus they begin to establish a relationship immediately with the new life. Another traditional custom that some tribes still practice is placing a part of the newborn's umbilical cord in a special small pouch. This pouch stays with the infant and is believed to provide protection, good luck, and good health for the infant.

It has taken a while for Sacred Time to become profitable, but that is partly because of the uniqueness of my business. What I provide is not goods that are consumed but rather service, education, and time, both to the family and to the community. My service also stands apart from what has now become standard practice in this country—that of birthing in a hospital and being expected to take care of a baby with little or no guidance or support. Another challenge that I face is traveling many miles to reach my clients. Because of the long distances to get to the rural areas I worry that I will not get to the client soon enough, when they may need me.

Being in the business of helping others doesn't necessarily reap the same benefits that are valued in the corporate world—money, prestige, influence. Unlike the "9 to 5" world, I define success by how many women I can serve and not necessarily by how much money I make. Although my business is not completely established, my heart is still in making my company successful on my own terms. The mission of my service, Sacred Time, is a life-long passion for the Native Americans and I would love to tell them the TRUTH and help them get back to their traditional ways of birth and raising their families. My vision is a commitment to working with Native American populations to bring homebirth traditions, and trusting birth, back into their communities. I feel that birth at home is an ideal way to restore peace and health to the First Nation.

From my experience and observation, American Indian women starting their own companies struggle perhaps more than others because, sometimes, they do not have the financial support or encouragement they need from their communities. However, if you have a vision and follow your heart, do not give up on your dream. If you want something badly enough, keep at it until it works. Your purpose in life will be revealed to you if you look for it, but you need " eyes to see and ears to hear" – once you find it, work at it with all of your heart... as if you are working for God!

Andrea Northcutt Miller

TRIBE: Cherokee and Creek (Southeast Region)

FAVORITE BOOK: *The Bible: New Living Translation, Life Application Study Bible.* The book to live by, it has Spirit!

FAVORITE QUOTE: *In His grace, God has given us different gifts for doing certain things well. So, if God has given you the ability to prophesy, speak out with as much faith as God has given you. If your gift is serving others, serve them well. If you are a teacher, teach well. If your gift is to encourage others, be encouraging. If it is giving, give generously. If God has given you leadership ability, take the responsibility seriously. And if you have a gift for showing kindness to others, do it gladly.*

—Paul - Romans 12:6-8

EDITOR'S NOTES: Andrea's husband, Brian Miller, is a gifted horse trainer. His business is called Flying B Horse Training. He trains many different breeds of horses at all different training stages. Andrea has a two-year-old, handsome, and very smart, male Border Collie named "Flame" who helps out at the training facility – he's her baby! Her immediate family (Mama (Dot), Daddy (Max), and brother, Barry, and his family) live in the Gulf Coast area of Alabama, where she grew up.

Andrea loves to be outside; although, she is more comfortable in the warmer weather! She enjoys beadwork, sewing, and making gift baskets for her clients. Andrea also loves singing in church and takes pleasure in spending time with her family.

Her future business plans are to establish her service and develop relationships to not only obtain return clients, but to gain new ones through referrals from very happy families. She is honored that God has called her to serve families the way she does. Andrea loves traveling to visit these families in their homes and she feels blessed to have the opportunity to do so.

Theater is spiritual. Spirituality is the basis of all acting. That's why Indian people make some of the finest actors. They can take the deep emotions that come from history, as well as their personal experiences, and express them in powerful ways on stage.

—Julie Pearson-Little Thunder

Feeding People's Spirits Through Art

Julie Pearson-Little Thunder—If an entrepreneur is someone who creates her own job, then there was no question that I could be anything but. For as long as I can remember, I've wanted to be a writer. Every job I had in my teens and twenties—waiting tables or being a temporary secretary—was always "their" work. Every spare minute I had I devoted to "my work" –writing. I wrote poems and short stories in high school, but in college, I discovered a brand new (to me) art form: theater. I was too shy to act, but I loved hanging around with actors and watching my theater teacher direct. I also loved reading plays, especially by playwrights of color.

Problem was, I never ran across any plays by Indian playwrights. I never ran across plays with Indian characters (believable ones, anyway.) So when I heard about The American Indian Theater Company of Oklahoma, I knew I had to join. I moved from Denver to Tulsa to work with the company, and after one more waitressing job, I was hired as Administrative Director. Despite my title, even in 1982, my salary of $500 a month, divided by my hours, was far less than minimum wage. Still, this was a wonderful time of my life, one of the first times when the work of my employer, and my work, were one and the same.

I met my husband, a visual artist, at a time when he was struggling. He sold his paintings to individuals mostly, and sometimes to galleries. When The American Indian Theater Company of Oklahoma closed, I became the sales and marketing department for my husband's art. Me—the writer with absolutely no business sense—suddenly wearing a business hat! Me, the shy person who dreaded talking to strangers, becoming a sales person!

It took time and some practice, but this change in my circumstances led me to discover that I could walk into a business, not knowing a single person, and ask, "Is anyone interested in looking at Indian art?" I found I could say "no" to the person who wanted to pay less than a painting was worth and keep looking until I found someone who would pay a fair price. I realized I could even ask for an advance from a gallery owner for a half-finished painting— money that would allow our family to buy groceries or pay a bill until the painting was ready. When the painting was delivered to the gallery, the owner was always happy with his or her investment. I could do all this because I believed in my husband's art. I saw that people were hungry for his paintings and the stories that went with them. It wasn't easy living on art sales, never knowing day to day or week to week whether we could pay our bills. But somehow, we were always taken care of.

Over the years, my husband has also helped me pursue my passion for Native theater. He, along with my best friend, helped me co-found a Native theater company. When we started the company in 1993, it was called Tulsa Indian Actors Workshop. Now seventeen years later, it is Thunder Road Theater. Thanks to the founders, actors and volunteers—through many ups and down, including my decision to return to graduate school in my 40's—it's still in operation. I've been fortunate to realize the dream I had in college: writing plays for Indian actors. I've also directed plays by other Native playwrights.

Theater and ceremony have much in common. Native theater requires people to come together for a spiritual purpose; everyone has to do his or her part so that the play will be successful. The process of play-making creates community.

A special bond is formed between those who produce a play and those who come to watch. This watching is not simply passive—the audience helps the play happen with its energy and attention, shaping the way it turns out in performance. Those of us who act or work behind the scenes neglect many aspects of our lives during production. But as theater artists, we also get a lot back. The play brings different backgrounds together in space and time, and afterwards, it's clear something has been changed, or healed, or rebalanced in the world.

Theater is spiritual. Spirituality is the basis of all acting. That's why Indian people make some of the finest actors. They can take the deep emotions that come from history, as well as their personal experiences, and express them in powerful ways on stage. Young people, especially Indian teens, really benefit from acting. Acting demonstrates how self-discipline and self-growth are tied together. You can't do theater without being willing to grow, spiritually and emotionally. I feel lucky to have chosen a line of work that constantly challenges me.

I still travel with my husband when I can and help at art shows. And I still take other jobs to supplement our income. Our theater company is not well known; our individual members are not famous. And our company has never paid anyone a living wage, including me. But we are now training the children and grandchildren of people who first acted, volunteered, or came to watch Native theater in Tulsa in the mid-seventies. We are giving back to the community, and feeding people's spirits through art. Is that what it means to be an entrepreneurial success? Maybe not in the dominant society, but in the Indian country, yes.

Julie Pearson-Little Thunder

TRIBE: Myskoke Creek

FAVORITE QUOTE: *If a woman carries her own lantern, she need not fear darkness.* —Hasidic

SOCIAL MEDIA: FACEBOOK: Thunder-Road-Theatre-Co; TWITTER: Thunder_Rd

WEBSITE: web.me.com/thunderroadtheater/

EDITOR'S NOTES: Julie Pearson-Little Thunder is a playwright whose works include *Indian Meadowlark, Good Person of LA, Standing Up Stories, Woman who Was Captured by Ghosts and Gallery Buffalo*. As former Artistic Director of Thunder Road Theatre, she has directed over ten plays for the company in various venues in Tulsa and other Oklahoma communities. She has been involved with

Native theatre since the 1980s when she moved from Denver to Tulsa to work with J.R. Mathews and American Indian Theatre Company of Oklahoma.

Thunder Road Theatre is the longest-running Native theater company with multiple members who are not related by blood. Thunder Road is a community-based theater company drawing upon theater workers from Tulsa and northeastern Oklahoma and a predominantly Indian board of directors. TRT's mission is to present quality works by contemporary Native playwrights and to train Native Americans in acting, directing, playwriting and technical theater. They are an inclusive group that welcomes anyone interested in Native cultures. Live theater can help effect social change and serve as a bridge of understanding between the Indian and non-Indian communities.

My dreams are kept alive from the inspiration and teaching of my grandparents and God.

—Tonya June Rafael

Believe in Your Dreams

Tonya June Rafael—Ya ah teeh! My name is Tonya June Rafael. I am Dine of the Navajo Nation. I currently reside in my childhood town of Prewitt, New Mexico. I was born on June 14, 1968 in Gallup, New Mexico, to Lucy Rafael and Johnny Beasley Yellowhorse "out of wedlock." Lucy was not quite ready to be a mother, so she gave the full responsibility to my grandparents, Tom and Mary Rafael, to care and raise me when I was only two weeks old.

My grandparents had a busy lifestyle already. My grandfather worked politically with the Navajo Tribal Council, and both were involved with many traditional ceremonies in the community. They also had farm responsibilities, tending to their land and sheep. In the 70's, they began making their silver jewelry and travelling many miles to sell their work. We would travel to far places like Phoenix, Arizona, Oregon, Utah, and California to sell their handmade jewelry. We would also go to fairs such as the Navajo Nation Fair, Laguna Feast, Jemez Feast, Gallup Flea Market, and the Gallup Inter-tribal Indian Ceremonial to sell food and handmade crafts. My grandfather would set up the stand and sell his handmade crafts. My grandmother and I worked as a team in our food stand. She was the cook and I was the server. We would sell mutton stew with fry bread, coffee, sodas, hamburgers, and her famous Navajo tacos. I always looked forward to these fairs. I never saw it as work but as fun.

My first personal experience as an entrepreneur came when I was about seven years old. My grandparents and I were selling jewelry in Arizona at the Grey Hound Park swap meet. There, for only a quarter, I bought a tin cup with two matching spoons. I sold them for a dollar that same day. I was surprised and ecstatic that I had made an extra 75 cents. My understanding of how to turn a profit began to flourish.

I always watched when my grandparents hammered, stamped, soldered, and buffed their silver jewelry. When I was about 11 years old, I snuck into my grandfather's shop while he was taking a lunch break. My curiosity grew when I saw all kinds of silversmith tools and sterling silver designs sitting on the workbench, ready to be soldered. I decided to try on my own. I ignited the acetylene torch and started to melt my grandfather's work, but soon it melted into nothing more than a quarter-sized ball. I knew immediately I was in trouble. In fear, I threw the smelted silver ball under the workbench. My grandfather never knew what happened to his work. This curiosity of mine, however, led me to learn as my grandparents patiently showed me and encouraged me—"like this," they would say. I smoothed out rough edges of silver with a file, sorted turquoise, and cleaned jewelry in preparation for my future.

I began my career selling Indian jewelry at retail stores. One of these stores was my father's Indian gift curio shop, Yellowhorse Trading in Lupton, Arizona, a tourist attraction at the New Mexico and Arizona state line. Here I gained more experience in Indian jewelry making and sales. For three years following, I did "piece work" for a jewelry manufacturer in Gallup, NM. Piece work is done at home, so together my first husband and I would follow a sample, making around 100 rings a week, or at other times about 50 bracelets per week. For our efforts, we were paid only 75 cents per ring, or perhaps $1.50 if it was a bracelet. This practice of paltry pay to local silversmiths continues even today.

My background and early jewelry experience allowed me to work as a production manager at a jewelry manufacturer. This business frustrated me because even though I designed and developed the ideas, as an employee I was entitled to only a small portion of the profits. An even bigger source of frustration for me at this time was my first husband's alcohol problems. We now had three children, and the abuse became unbearable. I needed to escape this dangerous situation; now I had to protect and provide for my children alone.

I had always dreamed of owning my own business, but I didn't know how to get started. The one thing I did know was that I needed capital. But at this time in my life, I was at full-time student, and it took every resource I had to keep my family out of poverty. My children and I would sell on weekends at flea markets and at the train station in Albuquerque. I would buy "lower end" jewelry at wholesale and double my price for profit. It kept food on the table, paid the rent, and clothed my children. I sold even on windy, hot summer days and frigid weather.

I managed to save enough money to buy silver and silver supplies so that I could begin to make my own jewelry.

Using some of my grandparents' silversmith tools, I made my first pin pendant. It was an oval turquoise surrounded by pear-shaped spiny oysters. It sold at the Gathering of Nations Pow Wow for $200. Again, I was surprised and ecstatic. Little by little, I purchased sterling silver and various stones. I made more pin pendants, then rings, and earrings. I would set up at Pow Wows and at Pueblo Feast days and sell my work. My love of having my own business grew faster than my small inventory.

My older brother Lynol Yellowhorse also had an influence in my jewelry business. He was a renowned artist and maker of exquisite inlaid jewelry. He was the one who guided me into the world of juried art shows. Gradually, I exhibited my art work at various art shows in Arizona, New Mexico, and Oklahoma. My work has also been displayed at the Smithsonian Museum of the American Indian both in Washington, D.C. and New York City.

In the summer of 2004, I purchased some silver plate and wires. I prayed profoundly and asked God for guidance and creativity. A vision of a beautiful sterling silver purse came to me. So I made my first sterling silver purse studded with 300 cabs of turquoises. It was unbelievable that I could make such a piece. In 2005, the first purse I made won first place in the juried competition at the Eiteljorg Museum Indian art market in Indiana. Since then, I've made 35 different shapes, styles, and sizes of purses and won several awards at various juried art shows around the country. Prices on the silver purses ranged from $2500 to $8000 and every one of them sold!

The downward economy in the U.S. had an effect on my jewelry business. Silver prices rose tremendously in the winter of 2010, and jewelry production slowed. I was forced to raise my prices in order to profit from my work. To accommodate reluctant customers, instead of making larger pieces with higher prices, I made smaller, affordable pieces under $100 to keep the flow of business. This strategy has proven successful.

In the future, my dream is to display my art in my own retail stores in several New Mexico towns. I would also like to open a business school for Native women to teach them skills that will put them on the path to self-sufficiency. These are still dreams, but I will continue to aim toward making them a reality.

I have met so many wonderful people in this business. Positive and encouraging feedback from my customers and art colleagues has enhanced my abilities in the business and art of jewelry-making. While it is true that occasionally I have been faced with colleagues or acquaintances who try to spoil my vision, my dreams are kept alive from the inspiration and teachings of my grandparents and God.

Tonya June Rafael

TRIBE: Navajo

EDITOR'S NOTES: Tonya says that she would have never succeeded with her business without God in her life. She is also thankful to her husband Gabe; her beautiful children,

Stephen, Elizabeth, and Sophia; her brother Lynol; her chei and shi mom (her grandparents); and many of her wonderful friends who supported her. Ahe'hee!

Recognize and learn from the accomplishments among your own—seek role models in your own communities.

—Veronica E. Tiller

Tiller Research, Inc.: History as an Unlikely Business

Veronica E. Tiller—"I have to get back to College Park to teach my class," Fred informed me as he grabbed his old leather briefcase and rushed out of the National Archives central reading room. Professor Fred Nicklason was teaching American History at the University of Maryland while also conducting historical research in support of Indian natural resource litigation through his Washington, D.C. private research firm. To me, Fred had an ideal profession where he used his knowledge of history as the basis for his business. He was my role model as I started my company, Tiller Research Inc. (TRI), using American Indian history as an unlikely foundation.

At the time I founded my company, I was teaching American Indian History at the University of Utah in Salt Lake City. While I was teaching, I served as an historical expert witness in the *Merrion-Bayless* case then in the U.S. District Court. That case went to the U.S. Supreme Court to establish that Indian tribal governments had the right to tax energy companies conducting business on Indian lands. I had nothing to do with the ultimate success of this case, but it opened the door to establishing my business. In the fall of 1979, I resigned my teaching position, and by December, TRI was incorporated in the District of Columbia.

I was convinced that I could make a greater contribution to Indian tribes by conducting historical research on their behalf than by teaching. My business goal was to be of service to the greater national Indian community and my own tribe. In the early 1980's, TRI obtained work mainly from D.C. law firms representing Indian tribes in their claims against the federal government for the mismanagement of their natural resources. TRI's first sizeable contract was conducting historical water rights research for the Rocky Boy Cree of Montana. Up to the mid-1980's, TRI's client list included tribes from Arizona, New Mexico, Colorado, California, North Dakota, Minnesota, and even a Canadian tribe from Alberta.

However, by 1986, the litigation support contracts were becoming scarce, and TRI was on the verge of closing its doors. But I was not ready to relinquish my plans for my company. With literally $200 in TRI's bank account, I doggedly went before my tribal council to convince the members to celebrate the 1887 Executive Order establishment of the Jicarilla Apache Reservation and to give my firm the contract to coordinate the activities. This proposal was, by far, a long shot, as my tribe had no plans to commemorate its centennial, but TRI was indeed awarded the project. TRI placed the Old Jicarilla Apache Agency site on the National and State Register of Historic Places. I also convinced New Mexico Governor Gary Carruthers to officially proclaim February 11 as Jicarilla Apache Day. Today, my tribe celebrates Jicarilla Week during the week that includes February 11.

It was this contract that got TRI back on its feet and taught me that I had to diversify my business services. I had to adapt to the situations and needs around me. TRI went on to work for the Jicarilla Apache Nation on a wide range of issues and projects, including historical water rights research, as well as conducting nationwide inventories of tribal arts and artifacts. TRI has also assisted in the collection and compilation of oil and gas-related materials to establish a records database in support of the federal claims case *Jicarilla Apache Tribe v. U.S.* (2002). Currently a project of high priority for TRI is the preservation of the Jicarilla Apache language. This involves developing multimedia curriculum materials for use in the community and schools and collaborating with a software company to develop voice recognition software for use by all Apache tribes and people. These two efforts will assist especially in the further documentation, preservation, and maintenance of the Jicarilla Apache language, which faces extinction within two generations if serious preservation efforts are not made.

Serving Indian Country continued to be the focus of my business, when in 1994, I established BowArrow Publishing Company as a division of TRI. The publication of the monumental reference guide entitled *Tiller's Guide to Indian Country: Economic Profiles of American Indian Reservations* was a direct response to the need for updated, accurate, and reliable information on all 562 Indian tribes' economies and businesses. It was published in 1996 and again in 2005. This award-winning publication is now considered the premier guide to Indian Country.

From my experiences, I have found that American Indian-owned businesses are unique in that they provide goods and services to Indian Country in a way that goes beyond the profit motive. American Indian-owned companies take on work on behalf of their tribal communities, often at discounted rates or even without compensation. Many times their priorities are business projects that are socially, culturally, and economically beneficial to the tribes. Frequently Native entrepreneurs create businesses that serve specific needs, such as in areas of welfare, juvenile justice, environmental protection, and language preservation.

The critical factors for success among Indian women (and for that matter, any person wanting to start a business) are the willingness to take risks and a strong sense of determination and commitment, because there are no guarantees for success in the business world. Flexibility and adaptation to changing business trends are also important traits.

As a beginning business person, I looked exclusively to the non-Indian community for my role models (i.e Fred Nicklason). It was not until much later in my life that I realized that there are many role models within our own Indian communities—we just tend to overlook them. Right under my nose was my own mother, who took over my father's ranching business when he passed away in 1954. She knew very little about the cattle business. All she knew was that she had to make a living for her seven children no matter the circumstances, obstacles, or barriers. She ranched on a remote area of our reservation and she had no office, no finance capital, no business plan; she did not speak in clichés about her ranching as an "entrepreneurial enterprise."

Sadly, I did not equate my mother with business know-how or view her as a business role model. When I think back, it was her determination and commitment to accept both the good and bad times, her willingness to learn about her business, and most of all, her hard work that helped her make a success of the business. Fortunately, her accomplishments were recognized by her peers in 1995 when she was given an award by our tribe for being a life-long and successful rancher. In retrospect, I have come to realize that I share all her qualities for success—determination, commitment, adaptability, and relentless perseverance. Without these characteristics, I believe that I would not have succeeded in my business. In the final analysis, these characteristics lead to achievement in any undertaking. And these qualities exist in abundance in our own Native communities and within our families. My advice for Indian women is this: recognize and learn from the accomplishments among your own—seek role models in your own communities. The private business sector in Indian Country is still in its infancy. Unfortunately, the majority of Indian-owned businesses exist outside Indian reservations. It is our job to recognize that Indian Country offers plenty of opportunities for Indian entrepreneurs, but the private sector will not grow unless Indian people, tribes, and communities work to give these endeavors our loyalty, promotion, and support.

Veronica E. Tiller

TRIBE: Jicarilla Apache Nation

FAVORITE QUOTE: *Be the change you want to see in the world. —Ghandi*

SOCIAL MEDIA: FACEBOOK: Veronica E. Tiller

BLOG: WritingNative.blogspot.com

WEBSITE: www.TillersGuide.com

EDITOR'S NOTES: Veronica E. Tiller, Ph.D. and CEO of Tiller Research Inc. of Albuquerque, NM today focuses on the writing of books on Native Americans and working with her tribe on its language preservation. Her book, *The Culture and Customs of Apache Indians,* was published in January, 2011 by ABC-CLIO. It is available from Amazon.com.

Chapter Three
Creativity and Life

If there's specific resistance to women making movies, I just choose to ignore that as an obstacle for two reasons: I can't change my gender, and I refuse to stop making movies.

—*Ramona Emerson*

Strength from Struggle

Ramona Emerson—A lot of jobs—bricklaying, sign painting, custom picture framing and forensic videographer—before becoming a filmmaker, but I think I always knew I wanted to make movies. My mother would take me to movies when I was growing up, and (after a lot of prodding) she took me to a Spike Lee movie. An American film director, producer, writer, and actor, Lee examined race relations, contemporary life, urban crime and poverty, and other political issues. I remember so clearly being only 16 years old and telling my mother my career goals. She did not discourage me, as one would expect, but instead went out and bought me all the Spike Lee films and books to help me learn how to be a film director. My mother was an artist and I learned a lot about odd schedules, creativity, and life. My grandmother was a huge part of my life—we also shared a similar passion for watching movies, especially Clint Eastwood and Charles Bronson films. Both women helped me become who I am today.

As I began Reel Indian Pictures, one of the challenges I faced was the scary feeling of not having a steady income. I was overwhelmed to realize that I needed to know all of the processes of the business—accounting, advertising, networking, relationship building. As a Navajo, I was always taught not to brag about myself so it was difficult at first to promote myself. Changing that behavior was tough. I had to learn to promote my skills and be proud of them in order to get business. I also had a good boss who gave me the tools to help me build a business. I worked to find all the people with knowledge in filmmaking, and I asked for advice. I went to everything I could to learn about the industry, read every book I could find, and watched all the movies I thought would help me learn the process of filmmaking.

Compared to other business cultures, American Indian business seems to be more community-oriented. I find it difficult to get or ask for money when taking on jobs where I know programs don't have money. Many times I do pro bono work to help out the clients or to just be part of an important story. It is vital for me to contribute to the communities in which I work; knowing I have to wait two or three months before I get a paycheck can be difficult, but the end result is always rewarding. I enjoy being part of their lives, part of their stories.

My husband and I have been working together for over 16 years. In this tough economy we do whatever we must to keep the business going. Sometimes we worry about where our next job might come from, but we always seem to get another. I know that there are people on the reservation who are struggling—certainly much more than I am. When we work with communities, especially children, it feels good to have them as part of our film teams—our crew. We are part of the same Native community and it feels great to know that there is a whole generation of Navajo children who are just as passionate about filmmaking as we are.

When I see children who are passionate and excited about filmmaking, it is important that they are surrounded by people like them who have the same interests. It is important to validate their interests and foster the dreams they have. For me, working with Native youth does that—and it gives them the tools they need to be better filmmakers. Learning hands-on is always best. There are so many horrible things happening in Native communities (high suicide rates, poor education and health care, severe poverty, violent crime, and drug and alcohol abuse), and children need to know there is more out in the world. Giving them a skill or a passion is even more important.

Our business is in its early years. After having the same job for over ten years, I found it difficult in the beginning to make a smooth transfer from being dependent on others to becoming independent and risking going out on my own, without the steady paycheck. We sometimes wait months for payment on projects. Over the course of this transition, I had to work hard to keep my confidence in myself. I am also still learning about the details of running a successful business—the paperwork, the accounting. It is sometimes daunting. But it is most important to do quality work and to maintain my commitment to community building through film and media.

Today I am able to stand on my own. I remember those, like my mother and grandmother, who supported me, and I gladly help others who need a chance to start anew or any aspiring or novice filmmakers who just need to get that first step in the door.

Ramona Emerson

TRIBE: Navajo

FAVORITE BOOKS: *Where the Wild Things Are* by Maurice Sendak; *The Prophet* by Kahlil Gibran

SOCIAL MEDIA: FACEBOOK: Reel Indian Pictures

WEBSITE: www.reelindianpictures.com

EDITOR'S NOTES: Ramona Emerson is a filmmaker originally from Tohatchi, New Mexico. She received her degree in Media Arts in 1997 from the University of New Mexico (one of the first two graduates of the program) and has worked as a professional videographer, writer and editor for over ten years. Her screenplay, *The Backroad,* was one of the first 10 finalists at the Flicks on 66 Digital Shootout (now Duke City Shootout), in 2000. The film, which was shot and edited in six days, was awarded the Student Spirit Award at the Indian Summer Film Festival in 2003. Emerson, who also directed *The Last Trek*, has showcased her films around the country with her latest film *A Return Home* being funded through the All Roads Film Project and New Mexico Governor's Cup Short Documentary Competition in 2007. She and her husband, producer/actor/artist Kelly Byars (Choctaw) continue to produce films through their company Reel Indian Pictures in Albuquerque, New Mexico. Emerson also works as an editor and director of photography on other independent productions. She is also the video production manager for Albuquerque Legal Photo Services, a firm specializing in providing forensic/legal evidence documentation.

Gambling with Our Future, a documentary produced by Reel Indian Pictures, was funded through the New Vision New Mexico Contract Awards. Ramona is also directing *Hidden Talents*, a documentary about Navajo mural painter James King Woolenshirt, with fellow Navajo filmmaker Nanobah Becker, who is producing along with the Shiprock Performing Arts Center. She is a member of the Native American Producers Alliance and in January 2009, was appointed to the New Mexico Governor's Council on Film and Media Industries. In May 2010, Ramona received the Sundance Ford Foundation Fellowship and attended the Native Film Lab in Mescalero, New Mexico where she is in the process of working on her new screenplay, "Opal."

Beyond her work as a filmmaker, Ramona and her team strive to teach Native youth about the importance of media in their evolving world. At Reel Indian Pictures, a strong Native voice is created through the medium of filmmaking. Whether through their own productions, or by passing on knowledge to Native youth, they are constantly looking for ways to give Native artists ways to learn the craft of filmmaking. This includes using film as a way to promote all of the arts - music, dance, art and acting.

As an awardee of the New Visions Contract Awards in the State of New Mexico, Reel Indian Pictures worked closely with the Native American Community Academy in creating a documentary workshop for 6th through 9th graders.

There's not a bad day that red lipstick can't fix.

—*Erin Merryweather*

Chicks in Charge

Erin Merryweather—My interest in art began with my first grade art teacher. She inspired me to grow as a creative artist and she believed in me. Today it is my husband who continues to inspire me and provides encouragement. I never really thought I would be in the business I am in today, but my degree in marketing and my experience in working in a creative environment after college helped me to build upon my artistic goals.

I started taking an interest in creating a venue for diverse and trendy styles of work when I realized my own artwork didn't quite fit in at the traditional galleries. After reviewing progressive shows by surfing the internet and gazing at every online gallery site I came across, I began to realize what I needed to do. At this point, it was no surprise that my dream was not only to provide a venue to feature my own work, but also to become an art business owner. It was also apparent to me that Oklahoma needed a unique forum for edgy Oklahoma artists to display and sell their work. I had experience working for non-profit art organizations; I had volunteered at—even chaired—different art shows, so I knew how things worked, who was buying, what was being bought, demographics, and spending behavior in general. I also studied trends in fashion, jewelry, and other accessories as well as watching clothing designer shows on TV and reading magazines that inspired me to take this journey.

At first, the idea of starting my own business seemed too big an idea to undertake. So I approached other artist friends for support and got inspired to put a team together. Coffee discussions with friends whose interests were similar to mine became a regular part of my weekend schedule. We started brainstorming ideas, our goals, our dreams, and the challenges we were sure to face. The same thought crossed our minds, realizing that this town could be a trendy, happening place just like LA, New York City, or Chicago. Oklahoma City could make a statement, and so could we!

Owning a business is such a labor of love in the first place that anyone with passion can make it happen. All you really need is a little business savvy and a good plan, and an executive team to grow your own company.

What started as just a dream became "The Girlie Show!" "The Girlie Show" is art, creativity, craftsmanship, and funk. Hand-designed … sometimes refined … and all by chicks. It's not stuffy like an art show or fluffy like a craft show. Think less haute, hotter. Guys, girls, good times. And this year is rockin' Number Eight (2011).

We decided to model "The Girlie Show" to fit to Oklahoma demographics, interests, and value systems because we wanted our friends to show their work in the state of Oklahoma.

Typically, a nice, neat little description would go here— something that tells you all about "The Girlie Show" and what you can expect. But you see, that's the problem. You never really know what to expect from "The Girlie Show." That's the idea that started this whole thing—"Randomness with a Reason." But for those of you who've never been, we offer you our best attempt at verbal seduction.

The first year each of my friends and I had a booth, but it has grown so much over the last seven years that now we are the organizers and hostesses. The first year we had over 800 people attend. Now there are over 2,200 in attendance! There has been a waiting line every year to get in the door. We were fortunate to have a lot of community support to help make the event a success. Since we did not have any data as a first-time business endeavor, we had to figure out other methods of selling the idea to artists and convince them it would be successful. Marketing was a key, and we needed start-up costs. Our goal was to select at least twenty artists during the first year to make a good showing, but even by the second year we had to turn artists away. We have now expanded to forty-five artists.

The team thought about moving the event to a larger place—and we did the second year to accommodate the growing crowd and increased vendors. But we believe that the ambiance of the original site is what helps sell the event. The event is held in a historical building. The historical gallery location has bright open spaces and high ceilings and lures visitors in for a look—both new and seasoned shoppers. Location is important; it enhances our vision. The artists also are energized by the theatrical, historical setting.

The result is a unique, vibrant experience for our guests and artists. The first show featured artists from Oklahoma and Texas. Now, not only emerging new artists from Oklahoma are juried into the show, but women participate from Seattle, Kansas City, Chicago, Austin, Montana, and California. Art work includes media such as paintings, pottery, sculpture, and pop art. Artists are not restricted to the usual jewelry, accessories, photography, and clothing. While the show features work by more than forty female artists, the event also includes food by local restaurants and entertainment by up-and-coming musicians and performers.

We have experienced considerable growth and development over the past seven years, including the addition of a $1,000 art scholarship, live band performances, and community involvement. When the recession hit, we didn't know what to expect and were surprised that this past year went as well as it did. We all worked to reach out to a wider audience: "You stop, park and shop. We have the variety and quality."

Perhaps no one has helped put "The Girly Show" on the map more than the team. I concentrate 100% on marketing, artist development, and administration while the other team members focus their time and expertise on advertising, media relations, and graphic design. What was not that hard was gaining support from local businesses. We began looking for sponsorships, and I met with my contacts and networks. I was fortunate to be good friends with an editor of a magazine. He promoted our first event to help us get recognized and even put us on the cover of an issue. One challenge was getting the word out to other artists to take a risk in joining our efforts, paying the entrance fee, and getting people to participate.

Networking is a huge part of why we are successful. Another is the concept of perceived value: both purchasers and artists feel that they are getting something wonderful in return for their efforts. This concept is significant in artists being successful. If you don't price yourself for what you are worth, you do not share in the perceived value. It is often hard for artists to see their worth. For an individual to deliver value, one has to grow her knowledge and skill sets to showcase benefits delivered in a transaction, such as pricing one's items at what they are worth and really getting paid for a job.

The perceived value is also a parallel between art pieces and consumer expectations. For an organization to deliver value, the key is ensuring that the customers believe that what we are offering is beyond their expectations, making them happy and creating positive energy between the people and the artists. "Good energy" is what many customers are looking for in the coming season.

"The Girly Show" includes the reputation of the organization, staff, artist representation, and product as compared to competitors' market offerings and prices. Perceived value can thus be defined as the relationship of our company's market offerings to those of our competitors.

Too often we allow the events in our lives to become detours and roadblocks, keeping us from following our dream. If you have a passion for art and creativity that you want to share with others, then just do it.

Erin Merryweather

TRIBE: Choctaw Nation

SOCIAL MEDIA: FACEBOOK: The Girlie Show OKC; TWITTER: thegirlieshow

WEBSITE: www.thegirlieshow.net

EDITOR'S NOTES: Erin Merryweather is currently the 'Chick-in-Charge' at *The Girlie Show OKC* and Director of Programs at Red Earth, Inc. Erin majored in Marketing at Oklahoma Christian University.

The idea of *The Girlie Show* was born on a warm summer evening amidst good conversation and pink cocktails. Erin Merryweather and two of her girlfriends, Dawn Tyler-Harth and Marilyn Artus, made stuff but didn't really have a place to show it, sell it and work it. Their wares didn't fit the typical art show mold, but they weren't going to be landing in any craft bazaar any time soon, either. Hence, they came with an idea, 'Let's get this party started. And let's sell some arts 'n crafts there, too. Cuz there's probably a whole buncha girls out there like us, just waiting for a show like this.'

The mission of *The Girlie Show* is to give rockin' arts-and-craftin' females an opportunity to show their goods and make some cash in a fun party atmosphere. Yes, it's called an art show, but they encourage you to challenge the definition of 'art'.

Be willing to walk through open doors of opportunities and knock on those that are closed. Perhaps someone will hear you and open them.

—Jan Pruner and Bon Liesener

Ohana Artisians—
The Hawaiian Girls of the Southwest

Jan Pruner and Bon Liesener—Our mother tells us that when she and her sisters were little our grandparents would take them to a park called Thomas Square (still in existence today) and they would pick up seeds and seed pods from the ground. Our grandfather (we called him Tutu Man) would drill holes and polish them and our grandmother would string them into leis (long necklaces) and they would sell them to the tourists who came ashore from the cruise ships. Our grandmother's sister (Aunty Mary) would make both necklaces and earrings from seeds and shells which she, too, sold to tourists.

When my sister and I would visit in Riverside, California, with our mother who is full-blooded Hawaiian, a group of us girls would sit around the kitchen table and make jewelry. One particular time the youngest of the girls, Bon, was teaching Naomi, Tomi, and me (Jan) how to wire wrap semi-precious stones and make pendants. Bon had gained a few wire-wrapping tips from some close friends, but much was learned by trial and error. This new technique started each of us in a direction of creating jewelry for personal use, gift giving and even as a possible means of income. Tomi began selling her pieces locally in Riverside, California, while in New Mexico, Bon and I began making more pieces than we could possibly wear.

What began as a hobby soon grew into a sizeable inventory of jewelry pieces. We wore our jewelry and often got rave reviews by friends, local artists, and complete strangers who sometimes asked if we would consider selling what we were wearing. They were our *inspiration*. Our *motivation* came from the support and prodding of our spouses. They were funding our hobby and wanted a means to recoup some, if not all, the expenses that we incurred buying supplies for our jewelry designing. They were also as excited as we were about the interest shown by others in our jewelry.

This was the beginning of Ohana Artisans. Ohana means "family" in Hawaiian and our immediate family and friends would be our foundation, motivation and inspiration. Our business is very new.

Our first public exposure happened at a local hometown event called "Rio Abajo Days" in Belen, New Mexico, during the fall of 2009. We heard about the craft fair only a few days before the opening. As we debated about participating in the event, we began to assess our decision by using the *Pro and Con* approach. We found it easy to come up with all the Cons. The list looked something like this: The booth fee appeared high since it did not include set up assistance or tables and chairs; the length of time required to stay as vendors would be difficult since there were only two of us to cover the booth; preparation time was very short and we needed to inventory our items to ensure we had enough items to sell; and we were still undecided about the company name.

Our husbands brought insight to the Pros and helped to reflect on solutions. We concluded that the fee was a small amount to pay for exposure, experience, and expansion of our business; our spouses agreed to help with the set up; we could save on cost by borrowing or using our own furniture for displaying items. They reminded us that we had no problems in the past shopping at malls and staying on our feet for long periods of time. We also realized that there had been many times when we worked under pressure, with limited resources and within a short time frame; and we boldly decided to settle on a company name that day. Ohana Artisans—"The Hawaiian Girls of the Southwest"—is the name we chose.

So, we did it. The results were grand indeed! Although we did not make back our booth cost at that event, we did get the exposure we were seeking. The result has been a domino effect for us.

Our presentation at the fair brought rave reviews. Several people encouraged us to take our jewelry to Santa Fe, New Mexico, which is really a great compliment. The *Valencia County News Bulletin* editor interviewed us. A representative from the Valencia County Shelter for Victims of Domestic Violence invited us to attend an event as vendors and asked if we would be willing to donate a portion of our sales or some jewelry for their silent auction. We were honored to donate a few items. The interview by the local paper was published two days before our next event which was perfect timing for our new business endeavor.

As a result of that article, we are doing a lot of custom work. Our sales have increased and continue to double at each new event in which we participate. We now have a website that displays our jewelry at http://ohanaartisans.com and our future goals are to participate in events in Albuquerque, Santa Fe, and even Hawaii.

We have taught a few young people how to wire wrap, including a ten-year-old girl named Angelica. She sets up her own table at our events and sells her own creations. She also makes and sells earrings to fellow classmates, even taking orders from them as they make specific requests as to design. She is a young, but successful, entrepreneur.

We also taught another young woman named Ginger how to wire wrap and she has designed beautiful pieces with a style uniquely her own. She also sets up a table with us to sell her jewelry and other art work. We are pleased with their designs and excited to watch them grow their own businesses as young entrepreneurs.

One of our biggest challenges as Hawaiian women living in New Mexico is not being able to qualify as Native Americans for events that would allow us to present our jewelry designs among other indigenous peoples.

Our recommendation to other entrepreneurs—young, Native or indigenous, minority, women: It will take earnest effort to get out of your comfort zone but you can expect the greatest benefit when you do so. Be honest, fair, humble, and willing to support causes you believe in, work hard and love what you do. Things will not always go as planned but find the good in it and focus on the positive, be enthusiastic, and persevere. Be willing to walk through open doors of opportunities and knock on those that are closed. Perhaps someone will hear you and open them.

Jan Pruner and Bon Liesener

TRIBE: Native Hawaiian

FAVORITE QUOTE: Keep on asking ... keep on knocking and it will be opened to you. *The Holy Bible, Matthew 13:7.*

WEBSITE: www.ohanaartisans.com

EDITOR'S NOTES: Janice Pruner currently lives in Belen, New Mexico, with her husband, Doug. Jewelry design is a passion second to teaching others the value of Bible principles in daily living. She is a full-time volunteer educator, and the sale of her jewelry helps support her volunteer services.

Gwen Liesener got her nickname, Bon, when she was a little girl, because she loved the bonbon ice cream treats her father would bring for her. She currently resides in Los Lunas, New Mexico, along with her husband who owns a used car store, and her son who is now attending college. Designing jewelry is an art that she's very fond of, but, like Jan, her first and foremost priority in life is teaching others about how Bible principles can benefit them in their daily lives as it has done for her and her family.

Jewelry from Ohana Artisans can be found at "Gifts Galore" (Booth 12) in Bosque Farms, New Mexico. Also pieces are displayed at the Blue Portal Gallery in "Old Town" and Desert Willow Gift Shop, both in Albuquerque, New Mexico.

Sometimes I give things away, because I believe good things will come back to me if I do something good.

—Eva Hoeft

Repair, Reuse and Recycle

Eva Hoeft—The sights and smells of the general store intrigued me as a child. That pungent smell of new fabric beckoned me to that section of the store. Carefully arranged bolts of color—emerald green, brick red, marigold yellow—stood in stark contrast to the washed flour sacks from which most of my clothes were made. With twelve children in our family, "Repair, reuse, and recycle" was an unspoken motto in our home, so hand-me-downs and flour sacks were our common wardrobes. My mother would sew everything from dresses to boys' shirts. She would study catalogues to see the latest "fashion" and then make her own patterns.

I started sewing using a machine when I was eleven years old. I had always seen fabric projects in my home, with both my parents involved in making clothing. I remember feeling that a turquoise dress with two pearl buttons, made by my father, was the most beautiful dress in the world. So it was only natural that I wanted to make clothes for my younger sisters, especially their Easter outfits. Somehow my father came up with the money to buy some material, and not only that, but he bought me a pattern as well! I used that one pattern over and over to redesign and adapt to make blouses, skirts, collars, and even my brother's shirts. I remember making lined dresses, skirts, and blouse sets for many occasions.

Not only did sewing and pattern designing develop my creative skills, but sewing was a necessary contribution to help the family make ends meet. Learning how to work the sewing machine became an important step in my progress as a seamstress. The sewing skills I learned guided me toward finding employment at the Oshkosh B'Gosh sewing factory to make my living. The fine detailed work that I favor came once I was employed at King Industries. In fact, the greater efficiency of the sewing machine in this factory made it possible for me to "take in sewing" for extra money after the factory closed. While I was in the garment factory, I often did piece work, sewing such smaller, detailed parts of a garment like collars, cuffs, zippers, plackets for dresses, and the edging on jackets, which required hidden seams. While others considered this difficult, I enjoyed the specialized work.

In addition to sewing my own clothes in high school, I began to make doll clothes. I enjoyed the challenge of working with small, detailed items, and somehow I had the patience and ability to make quality items. This began my foray into sewing as a business. These doll clothes were sought after by my friends and family. While in high school I learned to crochet, and while not my favorite craft skill, I was able to sell my products later on to support myself and my two children.

My perfectionist attitude makes me a diligent seamstress today. I pay careful attention and am very patient, although this often leads to spending more time on a project than originally estimated. Since I am not always confident in my fabric selection and coordination, I often seek assistance with this and at times allow my granddaughters to make these choices. Often their selections cause me to think, "Really?" but their color combinations often work well together. Teaching my grandchildren the skills of sewing is important to me, although they may not understand at this time. Making a product is only one part of a business. You still have to learn to market, budget, and keep up with the trends.

I began selling at local and state craft shows years ago. Today my work is sold mostly by word of mouth. I make quilts, baby quilts, pot holders and customized towels. One of my obstacles or challenges that I have is pricing my projects; other vendors and crafts people think I tend to price my items too low. I have to consider the client or customer and determine what they can afford, especially in this economy. Deciding to sell at a lower price than what the items are really worth or not selling at all seems to be an ongoing dilemma I face regularly. Given the amount of time dedicated to each hand sewn item, I often short change myself financially. Sometimes I give things away because I believe good things will come back to me if I do something good.

Towels, potholders, and baby quilts are my top sellers today. People prefer my products because of the quality. I use the best fabrics and dedicate careful attention to each project. Especially in quilting, the fabric must consistently be of high quality. To mix high grade and low grade material diminishes both the quality and the look of a quilt.

True to my family's "Repair, reuse, and recycle" way of life, I have always saved scraps of material, buttons, and craft items. Others are quick to discard scraps, but if you stop to realize that your scraps cost just as much per yard as the original fabric, it makes you think twice about tossing them out. This saving could be considered by some as hoarding, but I see it as being careful and considerate rather than wasteful, and, while it may take a while, eventually I turn all that "trash" into a treasure.

One way I recycle scraps is strip quilting. Strip quilting, or strip piecing, is a quick and easy sewing technique using long strips of fabric sewn together in a pattern of your choosing. Sewing the strips end to end and then side by side until the desired length and width are achieved is a simple technique yet yields a lovely result.

These days I do a lot of my work by hand. This enables me to take my projects with me wherever I go. I continue to read about ways to improve my skills and spend time with veteran quilt makers.

No amount of protection of existing resources is too small. While most of us no doubt have a lifestyle more financially comfortable than my parents, it would behoove us to reconsider their wise ways for wasting nothing. Today's emphasis on repairing, reusing, and recycling what already exists is not new—my parents perfected it, and I continue to support that important value that protects our earth.

Running my hands over the variety of textures of each bolt of cloth in that store so long ago caused me to dream about the possibilities of what could be. The crisp cottons might be dresses for my sisters, or soft flannels could be transformed into shirts for my brothers. Each choice of fabric brought anticipation of something better—imagined and then created by me. This anticipation leading to creation is what I hope my grandchildren and others will learn and remember.

Eva Hoeft

TRIBE: Comanche Descent

FAVORITE BOOK: *Gone with the Wind* by Margaret Mitchell and Pat Conroy

EDITOR'S NOTES: Eva Hoeft is the mother of two children and has four grandchildren. Her hobbies include working in the garden and traveling. Eva wants to enjoy what she loves best, spending time with her children and grandchildren and sewing. Her company, Cozy Quilts, is located in her hometown of Oshkosh, Wisconsin.

Set aside a designated time in the day to work, and keep that time sacred, limiting distractions.

—Pauline S. Echo-Hawk

Native American Women: Know Your Own Value—Value Your Own Worth

Pauline S. Echo-Hawk—I come from a rich heritage of Native American entrepreneurs. My father was of the Wyam tribe from the famous Celilo Falls Village along the Columbia River Gorge. My mother is from the Palouse and Wanapum bands along the Snake and Columbia Rivers. For generations, the women of these bands and tribes have been—and continue to be—the driving economic force in the community. It is the women who conduct the ceremonial wedding trades, memorials, name giving, and general exchanging of food and arts. The women prepare for these events months in advance, making the necessary clothing, shawls, beaded bags, and other items to be given to each attendee. If the items are not made by the women, they are traded for or purchased. Many of these items received at ceremonies can be traded or sold and are often purchased by other community members. Thus, the women are vital to the preservation of the traditional arts and crafts within the community, as well as the traditional economy.

I learned the basics of traditional arts and crafts from my great-grandmother, Annie Johnson, when I was nine years old. We young women were taught plateau weaving, moccasin making, beadwork, and harvesting and preservation of traditional foods. In turn, we were encouraged to present these items to an elder in the community who was gifted in that particular craft. As a youth I did weaving, made moccasins, and harvested and preserved traditional foods; however, I concentrated on my school work at this time, so, much to my regret, I did not practice the crafts during those early years. Later, while attending college, I wanted to return to our traditional crafts, so I took apart a pair of earrings to see how to do a certain stitch, the peyote stitch. Because I was away from family who could teach me, this was the method of learning I used—trial and error.

I began doing beadwork mainly as gifts for family and friends. But as people saw the design and quality of my work, they began to purchase items or ask for special orders. I seriously considered opening a retail store to display and sell my work, but the cost proved to be too prohibitive. So I began to explore other ways to market my products. I joined a small group of twenty-seven non-Native artisans and crafters to establish a cooperative gallery in the small town where I lived. The Red Canyon Cooperative, I felt, would give me an outlet for my beadwork, keep my costs down, and help me learn as much as possible about opening and maintaining a store. The three years of training and knowledge I gained from this experience were invaluable. Through this opportunity, I came to realize that I wanted a more specialized market for my work. I needed to go where people were interested in Native American items and culture in order for my business to be successful. I saw the opportunity to sell my work at Pow Wows—events in which my husband and sons were already involved as drummers.

Products I offered for sale included beaded moccasins, traditional and contemporary beadwork, and plateau style cradleboards. Early on, I designed and made each item myself, later adding works done by other bead workers and crafters. To my inventory I added Native American music of genres ranging from flute to Pow Wow music. After a few years of these events and much travel, I set up an online business with the help of my daughter. While this website is currently in hiatus, from this experience I learned better approaches to marketing my business; I plan to get back online in the future.

From my experiences in establishing my own business, I have gained some entrepreneurial wisdom. While your time is your own to do with as you please, it is easy to let that time slip away on other details of life rather than to spend it on your business. For a woman, that time often goes to the needs of her family, relegating herself—and her business—to a lesser priority. It is important to find a balance between your business and the rest of your priorities. Since I feel that creativity makes us fully human, this balance is necessary for me because when I cannot set time for my work, a part of me is missing. Set aside a designated time in the day to work, and keep that time sacred, limiting distractions.

Native American women seem to struggle with saying "no," and this I see as detrimental to our business success. We need to maintain the balance of giving our time and resources to ensure success in business. While generosity is a fine quality, it sometimes collides with business decisions. Others will want to take advantage of your time or even your resources. There have been times when I have been asked for unrealistic discounts or impossible-to-meet deadlines. It is important to be firm in your decisions and not to waver. Know your own value and value your own worth.

My family has been the key to helping me discover my value and worth. My cousin, also a business owner and skilled bead worker, often reminds me to value my work. She has helped me develop my business sense and encourages my bead work through suggestions and support. My children are another support system. They remind me to "stay current" in such things as new technology and popular Native American music trends. My husband, too, offers a listening ear and asked-for advice. In the early years of the business, he supported me financially so that I could reinvest my earnings back into the business. Although my family members have found other interests and careers, I still consider them a crucial part of this business.

Take advantage of opportunities to research and learn about your business. Every experience—whether it yields a desired outcome or not—is an opportunity for growth and knowledge. All my "trial and error" experiences helped me improve both my business and beading skills. Over the course of these years I have gained enough skill and knowledge to recognize good workmanship and produce a quality product for my customers. My adherence to excellence has been recognized by the Natural Museum of Nature and Science in Colorado, where one of my cradleboards is on exhibit.

Today Native American women are still the driving force behind much economic success in Indian Country. We offer our communities inspiration, the qualities and skills of hard work, organization, and preparation while continuing to uphold and sustain the traditions of our tribes. We are rooted in our traditions even when branching out into new business ventures. We must not lose sight of our abilities and capabilities, but rather use our gifts to acknowledge, develop, and sustain our value and worth.

Pauline S. Echo-Hawk

TRIBE: Wyam, Palouse, Wanapum

EDITOR'S NOTES: Pauline Echo-Hawk owns Echo-Hawk Indian Trading Company located in Lyons, Colorado. She and her husband Walter have two sons, Walter Echo-Hawk III and Anthony B. Echo-Hawk; a daughter, Amy Echo-Hawk; and granddaughters Anaya Lamarr and Alexie Echo-Hawk.

Chapter Four

Spiritual Connections

American Indian women entrepreneurs have great opportunities to be successful even in difficult economic times. It means taking a risk of exposing yourself and your idea; it means allowing yourself or your passion to evolve as you move forward; it also means learning how to take and respond to constructive criticism, working to avoid taking it personally.

—Rose Twofeathers Hernandez

Healing Through Heritage

Rose Twofeathers Hernandez—How could a little pot of fresh basil betray my body? I was already in a vulnerable state physically, but the simple task of bending to pull a piece of basil laid me up and cost me two weeks of work that I could not afford to miss. I was not in a position yet with my own business to feel secure financially, so I needed my media technology job to support myself. My back problems left me vulnerable, and several incidents at work aggravated the situation. But the basil did me in. Returning home from yet another doctor visit, and fearing that I might lose a job I just started because of my health, I leaned to pick some basil on my own front porch, only to hear two pops and freeze in pain. I could barely move, and I was alone. The pain was so intense that it hurt just to breathe. To this point, I had been against medication, but I desperately followed the doctor's advice and took all of the prescribed pain medication. I spent my days in bed, weaving in and out of boredom.

One day I carefully got down on the floor, on my stomach, to pray. I vowed to my Creator and guardians that if I could have a full recovery, I would always make my art and healing gifts available to others in need at any time. I wouldn't ask for anything in return but, using my combined gifts, work to make another person in pain feel better, or even take that pain away.

I first started developing my craft skills at the age of four, taught to me by my grandmother. My interest grew as I learned from art classes in high school and the local community college in Houston. With creative art and media technology as my focus, I continued to explore artistic possibilities, particularly commercial art, taking classes in this area as well as working as an apprentice in a sign shop. I was fortunate to have the support of my parents and three teachers who encouraged me to pursue my career goals.

By the early '80's, I focused on Interior Design, moving to Portland, Oregon, to attend a private college. With degree in hand, I returned home only to struggle to find a job. Luckily, I could fall back on my artistic skills, working as a youth recreational director and teaching arts and crafts.

My knowledge of arts and crafts again served me well when I pursued yet another degree in Tucson, Arizona. I was able to limit my dependence on loans by using my previous education and experience working as a recreation leader and media technologist. I also sold my art at local festivals and at pow-wows to help pay for school.

In April of 1987, I began learning how to work with crystals and stones. Always willing to learn, I took a class in Crystal Healing from a psychologist and crystal healer practitioner, Carolyn Ball. Crystals and stones hold an intense amount of energy and have healing properties. The energy from the rocks is transferred to a person's auric field and then in turn brings about a balance and alignment to all the chakras (points of spiritual power along the body). The chakras become balanced with the extraction of negative ions or blockage of energies, often creating a noticeable lightness in the body. Through practice, I became skilled enough to present my work to a community with traditional healers in attendance.

Shortly thereafter, I was given an ancient reading of the Aztec nation. This communication with spirits, over 200 years old, is performed by certain spiritual and ancestral Aztec people from Central Mexico, and involves large red seeds or corn arranged in particular patterns. This reading made it clear that I was a Keeper of the Rock for my Mayan clan, meaning that I am the one who holds the knowledge of my ancestors and uses it respectfully in this century through my work with crystals and stones. I continue to honor that and remain close to my people in the healing ways. I have researched ancient techniques and tools of the masters and continue to use them today.

Around this same time, I taught myself how to wrap stones using silver wire. I then figured out that I could do more, like stringing beads and making earrings. I began to sell my wares at events like conferences, pow-wows, and art fairs locally. I enjoyed my work and even gained bit of financial freedom. Since then, I have travelled to Michigan, Arizona, Kansas, Missouri, and throughout central Texas vending my goods at craft shows such as my recent juried festival in Winfield, Kansas. I also teach my craft skills locally. So having experiences in learning, re-learning, teaching, and creating have made my work now almost effortless. For me, this is what entrepreneurship looks like—nurturing one's ideas and dreams and then working to turn them into reality.

I feel that I mostly give to others a sense of personal power, like trying to salve a sore that needs healing, whether spiritual, mental, emotional, or physical. My gift of healing using crystal and stone therapy brings optimum health to others. I have always considered my craft work to be a healing art form, so if I make beautiful earrings, pendants, or necklaces with the gemstones, the fact that the stones also benefit the person wearing them is a bonus. The other gift of healing requires a set of tools for therapy, so I do not mix the craft stones with healing stones. However, occasionally the crystal in a pendant can be removed so that wearers can combine beauty and healing, using the stone for meditation or in their own work. Periodically, I donate my services to people who need the work such as Native American or indigenous women, community activists, or struggling artists. Often people work hard to live their dream and need re-charging from time to time. I like being available to help.

Much of my business comes from non-Native people who just want to connect to "spirit." My work is "spirit" driven, meaning I just listen to what is being asked of me to create. All of my pieces are intended for the highest good and that alone brings a certain respect and acknowledgement to my work that is both gratifying and honoring. People want to connect to their personal spirit, and my being available to the public allows people to connect with me.

That connection is made and developed whether someone makes a purchase or just returns my smile.

American Indian women entrepreneurs have great opportunities to be successful even in difficult economic times. It means taking a risk of exposing yourself and your idea; it means allowing yourself or your passion to evolve as you move forward; it also means learning how to take and respond to constructive criticism, working to avoid taking it personally. Being a responsible entrepreneur is not just about creativity. It means maintaining financial records, paying taxes, having good business habits, staying in the loop of future events, and being available to do some things that you might not feel are worth your while. Sometimes I've had hardly a sale but gained a contact that proved to bring abundance later. Using the social networking tools or sites like Etsy or Facebook has helped me most recently. Following up with leads sometimes also proves to be beneficial. Recently, I gave a small pouch (with my business card in it) to a contact I met a year ago. The young man told me the business was pursuing local artists to make their goods and would most likely be calling me. Listening to that intuition can be a success factor as well. We must teach the next generation to use their inherent gifts to bring others a connection to their heritage. You never know how a new skill will bring peace to another, once shared or taught.

The potential for American Indian business ventures is as vast as the sea. We must support our own dreams and aspirations. Challenges like self- doubt, negative thoughts, or the physical and emotional strength to continue can often be barriers to success—I know they are hindrances to me. I best overcome them by giving myself a chance, creating goals and meeting them, asking for help from others when I am challenged most, and sticking to my overall plan.

Spirit exists in all of us and we of all people deserve the chance to be entrepreneurs as much as the second nation people. May we all be granted all the things to bring us sustenance, good health, and a good life as first nation people.

When you're unable to move your body for a while like I was, you are forced to analyze your gifts and negotiate with the Great Spirit on fulfilling your mission here on this planet.

I owe my soul to a bit of basil.

Rose Twofeathers Hernandez

TRIBE: Lipan Apache and Mayan descent

FAVORITE BOOK: *Grandmothers Counsel the World* by Carol Schaefer

SOCIAL MEDIA: FACEBOOK: Twofeathers Hernandez

WEBSITES: http://sitekreator.com/rosetwofeathers/main_page.html; http://www.rosetwofeathers.etsy.com

EDITOR'S NOTES: Rose Twofeathers Hernandez is a native Texan. She has been a visual artist since 1977 and practitioner in the healing arts for over 24 years. Rose has taught her healing arts to communities in south and central Texas and in Michigan. She conducts mini-workshops in the community and shares her technical skill of creating Native American medicine craft work and healing tools. Rose's art is available at the East Austin Farmers Market, in socially-conscious bookstores, gift stores, and at various gatherings of celebration and ceremony around her Texas home.

In my struggle with death, the in-out, in-out of my own frail breath patterns carried with them strength and a new awareness of love and life. With repeated rhythms, movements, steps, and breath, we at Dancing Earth seek to renew the earth and to recycle the patterns of life for the survival and sustaining of all creation.

—Rulan Tangen

Dance—The Breath of Life

Rulan Tangen—By 2002 I had danced as if my short, wide, brown feet were encased in the magical Red Shoes of Hans Christian Anderson's tale. I had danced from country to country, from ballet stages to modern dance studios, to pow-wow grounds. For more than forty choreographers, I had passionately devoted myself as an instrument, helping give life to another's vision. I had to learn to surrender my ego and embody everything and anything envisioned by someone else. And while these choreographies and characters mesmerized me and captured my imagination, I was waiting for the roles of my lifetime—longing for someone to create the dances that portrayed times both ancient and futuristic; portrayed characters mythical and human; recited oral histories all but silenced in the past.

What, then, was the moment that I decided to dedicate my life to the expression of my own voice and vision? What moment did I stop waiting for another to make the dance but step into the role that nature has made for all women: to be creator? It was the moment when I didn't think I had one more breath to breathe, when I thought for sure that those Red Shoes had indeed "danced me all the way to death."

I was lying fragile, hairless, and gray-skinned in a hospital room overlooking the Lincoln Center neighborhood in New York City, an area where I had studied, worked, performed, and lived for so many years. The "walk of fire," my radiation treatments, took place in another familiar area, Union

Square. The only movement I could make without pain and effort was a gentle rotation of my wrist and forearm, spiraling in and spiraling out. That was all the dance I had left, accompanied solely by the nauseating metallic of chemotherapy. I wondered, in the haze of reality/unreality, how much of me was dead and how much was alive. My body, once vigorous, was now no more than lifeless dust. I was reminded of indigenous creation stories of the origins of life emerging from mud, from earth, from clay, from dust. By re-enacting the creation story, I knew I could be re-born.

I shut my eyes. Shadowy figures entered the room. Ah, it must be my dead ancestors, relatives, friends. This must be how it happens, I thought. The shadows will lead me into the spirit realm. The shadows came closer and closer, and familiar they were, but I realized that the gentle dance to which I was being beckoned was not led by the dead but by shadow spirits of the living. I whispered the name of one friend, then the next, one by one naming all the people the world over who cared about me, who were holding me in their hearts, ceremonies, and prayers. As I barely whispered each name, overwhelmed by their love and the connection between all beings, my breath kept me going, infusing new life and strength into my weary body.

Less than a year later, I was invited to be one of four emerging international choreographers for an aboriginal choreographer's workshop in Toronto. I had regained my ability to walk only a few months earlier, and I was excited about my first commission as a "real" choreographer, yet somewhat intimidated. My hair was growing back in an afro, and my body was still weak and unpredictable.

Call it coincidence, call it miracle, but out of the four choreographers present, three of us presented versions of birth or creation stories! Mine was a duet based on a creation story of two clouds merging, creating moisture to fall to become mud which then breathes itself into life. Within this was "The Naming," a five-minute dance solo that embodied my life/death/rebirth moment in that hospital bed. I still like to present this "love letter" of gratitude for life and relationships whenever I present my work at a new venue. I use this ritual to tell others of my origins as creator of Dancing Earth, my dance company, and to honor all those whose talents came together to make Dancing Earth possible.

As I began to develop my dream of an indigenous contemporary dance company, I wanted it to involve indigenous dancers, indigenous themes, and indigenous teachers and trainers. I also wanted it to reflect aboriginal collective leadership, that is, the empowerment of every artist rather than a hierarchy, and the allowance for a multi-tribal voice rather than just one tribal perspective (perhaps this is because I am of mixed cultures—a "mutt"!). And so Dancing Earth was created.

Dancing Earth has no operating budget. We exist from gig to gig. Most of the offers come for me to dance solo, and I stretch the pennies to include at least one more dancer and as many as twelve if possible. My priority is for fare wages for dancers, each dancer getting paid equally or on a scale based on how many dances they perform. Since there is no fee offered for choreographer or director, I, too, must dance to earn a wage. I also do the administration, promotions, and booking myself. The tight budget has required that I design lighting and costumes. This frugality gives us the opportunity to be ecologically conscious, since costumes must be re-made from used clothing or fabric.

My ultimate goal is for Dancing Earth to be a multi-faceted collaboration with Native participants involved in every aspect of a production. Whenever possible I do this, by asking favors, borrowing costumes or sets, or by trading with Natives. Because so many in my dance group are professionals in other areas, such as musicians, photographers, painters, and filmmakers, we are often able to rely on our own internal creative resources. When the time comes for that epic dance production, I plan to draw from a wide range of Native talent—from stage managers and massage therapists to graphic artists and aerial trainers.

My first mentor, Miguel Valdez Mor, a Mexican Apache of the Graham and Peridance dance companies, coached me to learn a phrase, and then do it without the legs. Then, he instructed, do it without legs and arms. So I would just be sitting on the floor with my torso thrashing like a tree in a storm in exact time and articulation to the musical phrase. It was a powerful demonstration that you can dance—indeed you can live—without legs or arms, but if you have a torso (that can breathe) then you can dance!

This lesson was poignantly highlighted for me one day when I was hobbling across Union Square to my chemotherapy appointment. I got caught somehow in the middle of the crowds and literally bumped into Homer Avilar, a dancer I had once been partners with in Europe. We stood facing each other—me gaunt and bald, him with one leg, having lost the other to cancer. We reconnected with a mutual understanding that only two people in our positions could; from him I learned the inestimable potential of the human body to express the dance of life, and that each of us must do it in our own way. It was after his amputation that he went on to have an incomparable career as a solo artist, working with some of the greatest choreographers in the world and dancing until the day before he passed.

In her 1991 autobiography, dancer Martha Graham wrote about "blood memory," a deep connection to our ancestors "which stretches back two or three thousand years." While Dancing Earth is considered a contemporary dance company, it seems that I am often stretching back, creating dances about times before the dawn of humanity, or perhaps the upcoming dawn of a new time cycle, as in the Mayan prophecies. Those of us in Dancing Earth create as a group, bringing personal stories, ideas, and themes that, once shared, become a part of the being of all participants. For us, it is dancing by, for, and of the earth. As in the earliest traditions of humans in every part of the earth, dances are rituals through which we invoke our relations with each other and with the earth; we depict heroic struggles and sweet courtships; we celebrate plants and animals as part of our food sources and spirit guides; we welcome the repetition of the seasons.

"Survival is repetition," notes Iroquois singer and composer Sadie Buck. In my struggle with death, the *in-out, in-out* of my own frail breath patterns carried with them strength and a new awareness of love and life. With repeated rhythms, movements, steps, and breath, we at Dancing Earth seek to renew the earth and to recycle the patterns of life for the survival and sustaining of all creation.

Rulan Tangen

TRIBE: Métis

SOCIAL MEDIA: FACEBOOK: Rulan-Tangen

WEBSITE: www.dancingearth.org

EDITOR'S NOTES: Rulan Tangen is the Founding Artistic Director and Choreographer at *Dancing Earth*—Indigenous Contemporary Dance Creations, recruiting and training outstanding young indigenous performers for collaboration and development of the emerging art form of 'Indigenous Contemporary dance', with performances in theater, film and 'all terrain' venues.

Rulan Tangen was recently noted in *Dance Magazine* as one of the *Top 25 to Watch*. Her lifetime passion for dance includes international experience in the US, Canada,

Europe, Mexico, and South America as a choreographer, performer, and teacher.

Her credits include ballet and modern dance companies in New York (Michael Mao Dance and Peridance), Vancouver (Karen Jamieson Dance), Santa Fe (Moving People, Dancing One Soul) and California (Marin Ballet), and appearances with the One Railroad Circus, as well as extensive yoga training, and pow wow trail experiences as a Northern Plains traditional womens dancer. In Fall 2009 her choreography was recognized by an appointment as Visiting Distinguished Scholar at Washington University.

With a compacts devotion towards the development of the innovative field of Indigenous contemporary dance, she has taught extensively in Native communities throughout the Hemisphere including projects under the auspices of the Native Wellness Institute, and the National Dance Institute.

As a performer, she has been featured in lead roles with most of the major Native productions including Raoul Trujillo's TRIBE, Daystar Dance/Dance, Minigoowezewin at the Banff Centre for the Arts Aboriginal Dance Program, CAMA Awards, Aboriginal Achievement Awards, Robert Mirabal's "Music from a Painted Cave" PBS television special and subsequent 80 city tour, and assistant to the Directors of BONES: Aboriginal Dance Opera.

She believes in this form of dance as continuing the link of culture from ancient to futuristic, and this culminates in her vision for *Dancing Earth*–Indigenous Contemporary Dance Creations, for which she is choreographer and director.

Her choreography has been commissioned by venues including the Heard Museum, Santa Fe Art Institute, Society for Dance Historians, Hemispheric Institute of Performance and Politics, Teatro Nunes in Brasil, Centro Cultural de Recoleto Argentino, Native Roots and Rhythms Festival, Santa Fe Dance Festival, Native Cinema Showcase at the Center for Contemporary Arts, Idyllwild Arts Program, Living Rituals World Indigenous Dance Festival, Toronto Harbourfront's Roots Remix Festival, Aqua Caliente Cultural Museum, and the International Aboriginal Choreographers Workshop. *Dancing Earth* was selected for National Museum of American Indian's award for *Expressive Arts* 2010.

Rulan is currently developing theater and film and cultural exchange projects that bring dance to serve as functional ritual for personal, social, and environmental health and harmony.

When opportunity is paired with determination and discipline, prosperity is possible.

—Sherry Echo Hawk Taluc

Connecting Two Cultures—
Strength in Sharing

Sherry Echo Hawk Taluc—My friend, Leah, was adopted by a non-Native community when she was young, and she grew up disconnected from her Indian origins. Later in her life, she discovered that she was Choctaw, and she began to pursue her heritage. In her search, Leah learned the significance of the shawl and wanted one of her own. I have heard it said that shawls evolved from the blankets women carried and wore in old times. Blankets have been an integral part of Native culture. Not only are they used for warmth, but blankets are an integral part of births and marriages and burial rituals. They have been used to pay off debts and to show gratitude. Shawls are used in similar ways. Like blankets, shawls have been made from many different resources throughout generations, and today shawls are made of cotton, wool, or synthetic fabrics, often edged with fringe or ribbon.

As Leah continued to learn about her people, one of the first things she did was buy a shawl and learn its purpose. Unfortunately, she paid $130 for one which was not well made. When I saw this shawl and its lack of quality, it triggered memories of plans my mother and I had to develop workshops focusing on American Indian culture. One of those workshops was on the making of traditional shawls, and this moment with Leah inspired me to invite a small group of Indian women to my home to explore cultural projects. Our first meeting was planned around shawls, visiting, and of course, eating. These gatherings came to serve a bigger purpose—they became our connection to one another and to our heritage.

The gatherings eventually dwindled until there were just two of us. But this gave me a chance to see a new direction in my life. I decided there was no reason why I couldn't make shawls on my own, create a business, and learn how to market myself to become self-sufficient. More than ten years ago I started in one room of my house, and today much of my home, garage, and attic space is needed to produce enough shawls to keep up with the requests. I sell mostly at American Indian events such as pow wows, conferences, and cultural gatherings. Many vendors I know barely make enough money to pay the vendor fees, but I have learned to pay the fees a year in advance, so I know that part of the business is taken care of. This is a success factor for me.

My prosperity, in part, must be attributed to the western culture. Even though I have worked in mainstream society most of my adult life and made my share of money, I never seemed to be able to save to get ahead. Many years ago, I spoke a prayer of desire for this learning, and I began to seek people and information that could teach me this skill. I wanted to know what wealthy people knew about money so that I could bring those skills to my own life. Then I met my husband, Jim, a non-Native. He was part of the answer to my prayer because he taught me about money management in our marriage as well as in business. Out of necessity, Jim learned how to earn and budget money at a very young age. He grew up with an alcoholic father and lived through a financially difficult childhood, a lot like many of our Indian people on reservations today. But unlike most Indian youth, by the age of eight, Jim had a paper route during the week and delivered groceries on Saturdays. He gave one half of his earnings to his mother to pay bills, saved one fourth, and had one fourth to spend. He still prioritizes his use of money in that order: pay bills, save, then spend.

For Indian people, prosperity and abundance results in sharing. I learned from my father to trust that Creator would take care of us, and that it is important for us to take care of others by giving away. Historically, we depended on the creator to guide us and provide for us, and we lived day to day, sometimes with very little, but we always had what we needed. We believe that we are entrusted with the earth and all it provides, and we are not to dominate it for our personal gain. However, this is where the roads of the traditional and western worlds must merge. Life is not as it once was, and we must find a balance between yesterday and today. Our people do not sustain their lives from the land anymore, so it is imperative that Indians learn business skills to survive—not just to make a profit, but to afford ourselves the financial freedom to give back to individuals and communities as our traditions teach.

Native American businesses can benefit from the influence of non-Native ways, but finding a compromise between these two world views can be challenging. At its core our culture is not materialistic, and this can create difficulties because the motivation for work is not money. We recognize the need for traditional items, none of which are available in boutiques or department stores. Even so, within our cultural teachings, there has never been a concept of mass production. When a need for an item arose, we traded for it, or we trusted that somehow that need would be met.

Individually-made items are labor intensive and are not always cost-effective. But Natives benefit because we know that what we make will touch the person who receives it. A shawl, for example, holds a spiritual connection, not just with the one who makes it, but with the person who buys it, the people who see it, and the spirits of all those who have come before us. I make sure my heart is reflected in each design I create, and I incorporate elements of Native spiritual beliefs and nature's vibrant colors to express the dignity, beauty, love, and prayers of my heart. However, while the customer is first attracted by the spirit and creativity of my work, those are not enough to ensure total satisfaction. When a customer places an order, it is imperative that I complete and ship the product as quickly as possible, but above all else, it is critical that my product is well-made. From a business standpoint, quality increases repeat business and referrals; from a cultural view, the quality honors our people; from a spiritual perspective, a well-crafted shawl honors Creator—like offering a respectful prayer. So it is the combination of creativity, quality, and good service that develops and builds a strong reputation.

Some of the lessons that are lacking in our Native culture are the determination to earn money and the discipline to manage it. Our traditional teachings guide us in our day-to-day living and prosperity for the future, but today many Native people seem to be disconnected from this. In the past, this kind of determination and discipline meant physical survival—drying meat for the lean months ahead, saving seeds for the next year's planting, preserving at all cost our spiritual ways, and caring for the earth for the future generations. Unfortunately, that way of life has not translated into our understanding of finances. Instant gratification seems to be the overwhelming view in our youth today, and sadly the gratification is not aimed at meeting the *needs* of the moment but more about satisfying the *wants*, with little thought of next week, and virtually no thought of next year.

In order to earn money, build assets, and prosper financially, young people need to learn skills not only to maintain what they have, but to reach beyond the life that they know. Education is one way for people to reach for new opportunities. A formal education is a productive way to learn skills, but it is not the only way. For those who do not feel that school is an option, my own experiences with my shawl business show that there are opportunities all around if we are willing to explore unexpected possibilities.

When opportunity is paired with determination and discipline, prosperity is possible. The Indian people's prosperity originally came within the confines of nature, but business is a very different animal, and we must teach our people new ways to "hunt" for success through good business practices. Rather than forsaking the traditions and values of either culture, we as a society should seek to blend and thus benefit from both those Native and western traditions that inspire prosperity and encourage generosity.

Sherry Echo Hawk Taluc

TRIBE: Pawnee Otoe Missouria

FAVORITE QUOTE: *Creativity isn't something you wait for. Creativity is something waiting for you.* —Donald Walsh

RECOMMENDED BOOK: *This I Believe* – Edward R. Morrow

EDITOR'S NOTES: Sherry is the owner of *Shawls by Sherry*. She continues to value giving back to Native communities. Sherry regularly donates shawls to fundraising projects like the annual Pow-Wow at Washington University in St. Louis. She has also helped her own tribe by creating a special edition Pawnee design for shawls to be worn at special events.

My vision of service has changed through the years, but I live traditionally from a place of prayer and sacred direction.

—Tina Sparks

Sacred Steps

Tina Sparks—I began my journey toward self-employment on a set of concrete steps. Those steps led up to the American Indian Center of St. Louis, but more importantly, they led me to Sherry Echo Hawk Taluc. I had just returned from my first Sundance ceremony in South Dakota. Sundance is a four-day ceremony of sacred ritual, dance, and prayer "so that the people may live." I knew that my lingering experience needed a purpose, so I went to the Indian Center with a desire to give back to the Indian community; I am amazed, still, at how much that day has given to me. I arrived with a full heart and my best lemon pound cake, and I left with what would become one of the most impacting friendships of my life. With what seemed like a chance meeting of two Indian women, sacredness seared our hearts and our paths together, and we continue even today to walk in a kinship of sewing and service to "the people." My vision of service has changed through the years, but I live traditionally from a place of prayer and sacred direction.

I began to teach myself to sew eleven years ago. My friends Jim and Sherry (Echo Hawk) Taluc had recently started a shawl business, *Shawls by Sherry*, and couldn't find a consistent source of ribbon work to enhance their creations. I saw a need, and took a chance—not because I knew how to sew, but because I had a need as well – to provide for my four children. I was in the process of a divorce and had started a job caring for a disabled girl and her family's household needs. The job paid well and offered some flexibility in scheduling, but work hours were limited. Life as a single mom was going to require more money than that job alone offered. Sometimes necessity really *is* the mother of invention. I held back a bit of grocery money to buy fabric, dug out my mom's old Singer, and decided not to be afraid to get it wrong. What did I have to lose? Just a few dollars' worth of fabric and a little bit of time.

When I showed Jim and Sherry my first two pieces, I quickly realized that I had missed the mark. I asked them not to give up on me yet, and I returned to the Singer determined (or stubborn) enough to try again. I bought some more fabric and invested some more time. My next few pieces were still elementary, but considerably improved, and Sherry was kind enough to buy them – maybe out of pity, maybe out of love, or maybe it was her way of encouraging me to keep sewing (she's tricky like that). Whatever her motivation, it was what I needed to keep me showing up at the machine.

I enjoyed the work, but drawing on my own artistic background, I began to explore other design possibilities. I happened to see one of Sherry's personal shawls with appliqué work, and I was inspired to try this new (to me) sewing technique. I grew in excitement and skill as I pushed past the limits of what I had learned and moved into unexpected successes in shawl designs. Orders started to increase and so did the financial return.

I continued to create large designs for *Shawls by Sherry* over the next few years, but again my artistic spirit grew hungry. During a trip to Albuquerque, New Mexico, my cousin Mike, a Purple Heart recipient, expressed a desire for a shirt he could wear when he spoke publicly on veterans' issues. My intention was to create a unique design that would not only honor his service to our country, but reflect our native heritage as well. I used the New Mexico state symbol (Zia, the sun) as the central image representing our ancestral land. In its center I placed an image of a Purple Heart to recognize his physical wounds from Vietnam. Two eagle feathers hung from behind the medal, mirroring the feathers that were presented to a warrior when he returned from battle with honor. The first few times he wore it to veterans' gatherings, Mike returned with requests from other veterans for me to make them shirts, too. Again, I saw a need and took a chance. This was when my entrepreneurial spirit was born. People kept telling me I had come up with something special, and after a while I began to believe them. I created more designs specifically to honor veterans but quickly got requests for shirts that expressed a person's connection to a particular animal spirit or reflected a personal spiritual experience. It was becoming undeniable to me that this was more than a chance happening; it was something I was being called to do.

As my work with fabric increased, my main income as caregiver was in danger of decreasing. With talks of a possible cut in pay, the uncertainty frightened me. But during a discussion with my employer, my focus was suddenly severed from the voice of my boss and redirected toward a new voice now in my ear—quiet yet firm, unexpected but not unfamiliar—it instructed, "Pursue your craft." I was washed with a sense of calm and an awareness of something bigger than that moment, weighted with all its worries. I recognized a presence so small as to fit in the absolute center of my being yet so immeasurably big and so tightly intertwined with my soul that separation was impossible. In that moment I was held in sacredness and reassured that I had nothing to fear because I was not alone. Returning abruptly to the conversation in the room, I quickly realized that I had missed some conversation of significance, but I left work that day cradled in the trust of Creator's hand in it all. When I returned to work the next day, I was told my hours and pay would remain the same, and over the next few months I actually had an unexpected increase in hours. I was certain that I would be safely provided for as I continued to "pursue my craft."

Time passed and my artist's belly began to rumble with creative hunger once again. The artistic hunger drives a curiosity that, if starved can kill the art but if fed can lead to amazing new recipes for creativity. I began an exploration of fabric paint to enhance my established designs and quickly found myself in foreign territory. My past artistic security was with pencil and charcoal drawing, and now, to a small degree, with a sewing machine; however, I had always been afraid to paint. Determined, I began to paint but was repeatedly frustrated by my inability to understand this new medium. I quickly found myself blocked.

Unable to *work* through it, I began to *talk* through it. I talked about it to anyone who would listen. I talked at the fabric store and the sewing center. I talked at the craft store and the art store and finally stumbled into someone who mentioned paint pencils. My eyebrow raised, my adrenalin surged, and I "knew" something significant had just presented itself. I didn't know what exactly, but that didn't matter, because I knew how to use a pencil! I so wanted to explore this new artistic territory, and the thought of taking an old friend with me was comforting. While the watercolor pencils would not be the total answer to my fabric painting dilemma, this bit of newfound knowledge was the next step on my entrepreneurial journey.

Despite my uncertainty as to how this was going to move my business forward, I stayed willing to take a chance. I thought I would find easy navigation on this journey with the comfort of my old friend, the pencil, but what I actually discovered was a new friend—water. Up to this point, I had only thought of water from the perspective of purpose—through thirst and human survival, through its necessity for ceremony and cleansing—but as a friend, not so much. After the first few days of this pencil-to-paint process, I became acutely aware of water's presence. Despite my struggle to put paint to paper in a way that made any sense at all, the water silently reassured me that I was not in this alone. I had unknowingly begun another sacred relationship, and I suspected that this process would be far more than metaphorical if I opened myself up to it – allowing the water to carry *me* for a while. Relationships have the capacity to do that if a person is willing. *Mitakuye oyasin* – we are all related.

I had no idea that paint would become a product of my business that stood on its own, but then I sold a print of an original painting to a complete stranger! This held significance for me because the motivation for the purchase was not out of love for the artist; it was strictly out of love for the painting and the person who would receive it. This painting, too, honored the dedication and service of a relative in the military; I could not help but notice this pattern of military recognition around which my business was expanding.

I come from a family with a long generational history of military service, and for the last five years I have had a growing concern for returning female veterans. I have often found myself engaged in conversations about how significant their injuries are and how unprepared we are to help them heal. Through my business, I am turning this concern into a commitment. I am brainstorming ways to incorporate traditional native craft work and art into healing arts that can assist wounded female veterans. These arts have always been a cornerstone of strength and beauty, of practicality and prayer, of communication and community for native women. My goal is to create a place for these women to rest in the arms of other native women, to release their pain within the arts, to reengage their womanhood, and to transition back to a society that has held a space of sacredness for their return.

As I have walked this path of ceremony and sewing, of service to the people and business for myself, I have remained open to the journey and its purpose. It has taken me to unexpected places, exposed me to diversity, and provided me with bountiful blessings. It continues to open new doors of creativity, growth, and direction – always merging the connection between sacred and secular.

Tina Sparks

TRIBE: Pueblo and Hunka Lakota

FAVORITE BOOK: *Power of Intention* by Wayne Dyer

EDITOR'S NOTES: Tina is a single mother of four—Justin 28, Jazmyn 17, Amalia 15, Autumn 13, and grandma of one, Colette, 11 months. Having put her college career on hold while raising her children, Tina is ready to return to complete her degree now that they are becoming young adults. She continues to pursue many forms of art, mostly self taught, and intends to incorporate them into modalities of healing for returning female veterans. Ultimately Tina would like to develop a transition program to house, heal, and help train veterans to serve society in capacities outside the military. In addition to owning and operating her company Sewing 4 the People, she speaks publicly on native culture and spirituality and does her best to educate people on Natives, past and present.

# Chapter Five

Connecting with Nature

Seek balance, embrace change, and above all, don't let the fear of falling keep you from soaring to great heights.

—Deanna Wohlgemuth

Down to Earth

Deanna Wohlgemuth—I didn't set out to have my own business. It was more of an evolution spurred by wandering down a path of self-exploration and learning to live authentically. Today I am the spirit behind Rock On Jewelry Design.

I began my career in corporate advertising sales. After fifteen years, I was exhausted and frustrated by the lack of balance in this life—nothing was ever enough. There was always more money to make, more time to devote, more clients to sign and sell. I began to long for a more sane existence, to get back to the kind of life I knew as a child. I didn't recognize it growing up, but my mom and grandparents were my first connection to Cherokee life, and while they didn't "preach" Cherokee ways, they showed me by example. Because we lived across the field from each other, I never knew a day without my grandparents. Through their farm, they remained connected to the earth and led a happy, balanced, simple life. My grandpa taught me to respect the earth. He showed me that there was a natural communication with the beings on the farm, and although there were always animals to feed, hay to get in, the garden to tend, and wood to gather, he always had time to share his music, laughter, and stories with me.

In my heart I knew those ways. But I was not raised on the reservation, so I often had the feeling that I was not "Indian" enough to call myself Cherokee. It was family who taught me that a person can't be a "little" Cherokee. Being

Cherokee is a way of life—it is in your heart. I became comfortable and more vocal about who I am as a Native person. I felt I finally had something to offer as a Cherokee and claimed my tribal citizenship in my 30's. I began to seek out Cherokee history and Native values to expand on my connection with nature. This led to my interest in Earth Medicine and stones and their stories. Sometimes the research would draw me to the healing energy that the stone possessed. Other times it was the lesson that I learned from working with a particular stone or found object.

As I gained my independence, the corporate world continued to take a draining toll. Meditation with nature and stones became an important part of my attempts to achieve focus and balance. Having a creative outlet became therapeutic. I carried different stones with me as a reminder to stay connected. Depending on the day, I might carry an Agate for focus, or a shell to remind me of the ocean and the constant ebb and flow of life. I learned to wire wrap to ensure that the stones could be worn without alteration or damage. The stones could now be seen by others. But rather than talk about the stones as art, I would share the story behind the piece and the connection I had with it. Soon others brought me stones to wrap, and with them, their stories. It became less about the jewelry and more about the connection to the earth and one another.

I continued to wrestle with the philosophy of the corporate world until I took a trip to Mexico to recharge and reconnect. There, surrounded by ocean, blue sky, and close friends, it became easy to see what was really important. It became clear that I wanted more out of life, but that "more" meant I could do with less. Living small and more sustainably would mean more time for life and my children. As we meandered through Mexico, I was drawn to a little beach shop owned by two sisters. The shop was full of items that held meaning and stories shared by the sisters. I remember feeling, *This is the balance that I have wanted for myself!* I made the decision that changed my life—I left the corporate world to reinvent myself, putting my energy, knowledge, and heritage into my passion. Thus, Rock On Jewelry came to life.

My business is now seven years old. It is eco-friendly in that I don't buy stones that are currently mined; I use natural shards that have been discarded or passed on to me. Beads are also recycled from old necklaces, estate sales, and gifts from friends. Rather than call it "Green" I prefer to call it "Red," for earth-friendly isn't a new concept—for Native people, it is ancient. Taking care of and honoring Mother Earth is a way of life passed down through generations. I honor those old ways through my work. The stones that I wrap are rough and natural, teaching us to be comfortable with our own imperfections. These pieces, found in abundance, tell a story, and it is an honor to be considered a storyteller of the earth. While my work is not traditional Cherokee, it is, nevertheless, authentic Cherokee. My business continues to evolve, and I am curious to see where it will go from here. But right now, my favorite aspect is the private showings and parties because it is here that women gather and share their stories. Together we value the jewelry, not as inventory or trinkets, but as a relational bridge, joining the earth and each other.

While I am more comfortable in my skin these days, the fear and doubt still creep in. Memories of a "real" job and a regular paycheck infiltrate my thoughts. It is a struggle sometimes to realize that I have worth even though I no longer have a title or sales awards to back it up. Now success equals quality of life and work, preserving my heritage, and sharing it. It has become increasingly important for me to be an advocate for this generation of Native Americans. We are not just part of the historical past. We are thriving, viable members of society with an ancient way of life that is relevant today. We must learn from our Native past, make peace with it, and use that knowledge to move forward in balance.

It is nature that teaches me the most valuable lessons, which I infuse into my work. On a hike up Beacon Rock in the Columbia Gorge, I was taught to overcome fear. Afraid of heights, I uneasily clung to the railing near the top to take in the view. A bald eagle flew overhead and I'm convinced we locked eyes. It was as if he was saying, "What are you afraid of? It's great up here!"

What I wish is that you find a path to wander, or several. Seek balance, embrace change, and above all, don't let the fear of falling keep you from soaring to great heights.

Deanna Wohlgemuth

TRIBE: Cherokee

WEBSITE: www.getyourrockon.com

EDITOR'S NOTES: Deanna lives in Portland, Oregon, with her two children, Willow and Cooper, and her best friend, Cory. She is a citizen of the Cherokee Nation, a member of the Cherokee Art Association, and a member of the Oregon Native American Chamber of Commerce. Her work is shipped world-wide from her web-based business getyourrockon.com. In addition, Deanna participates in Native Art shows, Pow-Wows, and sustainability shows. Her business continues to allow her to live the kind of life she treasures.

Keep your mind open to new challenges, a smile on your face, and be true to your word.

—*Lisa Kraft*

Generational Principles: Their Modern Application to Business and Personal Success

Lisa Kraft—I knew that I wanted to be an entrepreneur in the early 1990s when I was a student studying cultural anthropology at the University of Oklahoma. My husband and I had just met and were at different educational stages: me in my undergraduate work and him completing a Ph.D. To make ends meet, we became contract archaeologists. I still remember our excitement when we landed a contract to survey thousands of acres for a western Oklahoma tribe. Not only were we getting paid to do something we loved—being outdoors, walking the land, and looking for clues to the past—we were actually helping a tribe regain control of its history for future uses.

Shortly after I graduated, I was hired by my tribe, the Citizen Potawatomi Nation, to be its full time archeologist. The tribe was not soliciting, but that did not stop me from asking the tribal chairman if there was a need for me. I had an education that coincided with tribes asserting their legal rights under the Native American Graves Protection and Repatriation Act (NAGPRA). Tribes had fought for and received the ability to claim their ancestral human remains and cultural patrimony from public and private museum collections across America. I became zealous in my efforts and spoke in public every chance I got. Eventually, I earned the attention of tribal elders and the tribal chairman and became someone who could deliver on her word.

My grandmother, a very active member just like her father, helped me establish cultural credibility before her passing. When I came on as a tribal employee, her legacy was something I was proud to carry on—it also kept me true to my word.

However, within a year of my employment, the tribal chairman had set me on a completely different path. He introduced me to a brilliant woman who later became my son's godmother, my mentor, and one of my dearest friends. Together, we were asked to research the tribe's finances and internal programs for the purpose of negotiating all of the tribe's existing contracts with the Bureau of Indian Affairs (BIA) and Indian Health Services (IHS) into lump sum compacts.

Working together, we successfully negotiated multi-million dollar agreements with the heads of these federal agencies and brought our tribe into an exclusive membership of self-governance tribal nations. I went on to write numerous grants to enhance the tribe's cultural, social, health, and educational programs. When I left the tribe to pursue a master's degree in history, I had secured over $6 million in federal grants and contracts.

The study of American history broadened my mind and turned my attention to tribal politics. I discovered theoretical foundations that made me see how exhibiting history can instill tribal nationalism and inspire new generations of leaders. When tribes are not in control of telling their own history, their living members are often disconnected from the present and future. Since research has shown that there is a growing trend of tribal leaders and their communities helping make 21st century tribes one of the fastest growing sectors of venture capitalists in America, my aim was to produce a thesis blueprint for creating nationalistic exhibitions that would result in multiple generations becoming more productive, contributing citizens to their respective tribes.

Within months of earning my master's, I used my previous federal grant and contract experience to become a federal contracting specialist with the U.S. Department of Agriculture (USDA). Not only was the job a God-send for a recent graduate, but it afforded me a better understanding of federal grant and contract creation and administrative processes. I was very fortunate to work with two other women—one a senior contracting officer and the other a contracting specialist from Thailand. As a team, the three of us advertised, awarded, and administered multi-million dollar construction projects to clean up natural disasters affecting Oklahoma waterways.

The first time I saw my boss—all of five foot three inches—put on a hard hat and tell a group of fifty men how she wanted a new dam and reservoir built, I felt empowered. Later, when I watched my coworker and best friend do the same in her Thai accent and petite frame, I felt something akin to motherly pride. Our belief and support of one another allowed us to radiate success. We remain kindred friends to this day.

My boss had the hard-earned construction experience and federal contracting acumen to appreciate the federal government's small and disadvantaged business program, known more commonly as 8(a). She taught me the nuances of construction contracting with the government and how American Indian contractors and tribal nations could use their minority status to win contracts. I eventually left the USDA to become a federal grant and contract consultant and created Copper Bear Consulting, LLC, in 2006.

I carefully considered a name for my new business before making a final decision. I wanted to incorporate both the clan that I was initiated into (Bear) and the prehistoric currency of the Potawatomi or Great Lakes people (Copper). The former had been given to me early on to protect me during the work of repatriating ancestral remains from museum collections. The latter was more wishful thinking—I knew I would need both personal strength and money to make my dreams come true.

In just a few months of launching Copper Bear, I was awarded a consulting contract with the Citizen Potawatomi Nation. Having returned to my roots once again, I was asked by the tribe to convert 2000 acres of fee land into federal trust—an almost impossible task, but a challenge I welcomed. With tenacity and a fantastic tribal team, we developed a federal application and process within six months. Today, almost all of the 17 applications have been accepted by the Secretary of the Interior and the tribe has quadrupled its trust land holdings.

I feel that there is not a better way for me to make an impact on the youth of our tribe than to give them and future leaders more land use options. As the tribe's trust land base grows, so, too, does the ability to grow tribal businesses and expand services for tribal members. Just this year, the proceeds from tribal businesses and taxes have allowed the tribe to award just under $2 million in tribal member educational scholarships. This is up significantly since I received my first tribal scholarship almost 20 years ago.

In sweet irony, I had to give up my main tribal client (the Citizen Potawatomi Nation) when I had an opportunity to enter tribal politics in 2007. Lawmakers at the tribe cannot do business with the tribe due to conflict of interest. Two years ago, I sadly reminisced that I lost my consulting "bread and butter," but today I know that I am able to bring bread and butter to the tables of thousands through the jobs the tribe creates. I am blessed to be able to make programmatic and funding decisions for the ninth largest tribe in America with an annual operating budget of $300 million.

For those of us trying to grow our businesses while being wives, mothers of young children, and once again contemplating more education, I say keep your mind open to new challenges, a smile on your face, and be true to your word. In the end, dependability and true friendships will rarely fail you.

Lisa Kraft

TRIBE: Citizen Potawatomi Nation

FAVORITE QUOTE: *Character cannot be developed in ease and quiet. Only through experience of trial and suffering can the soul be strengthened, ambition inspired, vision cleared and success achieved. —Helen Keller*

RECOMMENDED BOOK: *Prodigal Summer* by Barbara Kingsolver

WEBSITE: www.copperbearconsulting.com

EDITOR'S NOTES: Lisa Kraft is the President of Copper Bear Consulting, LLC. Lisa and her family live in Oklahoma. She spends her spare time raising a small son, riding horses, living on the lake, keeping a written and photographic journal of life, and spending time in Denver with her sister, niece and nephew.

We all work together and depend on each other. This is how we live and work.

—Crucita Melchor

The Gift of Clay

Crucita Melchor—My mother took me with her as an interpreter when she was invited to Washington D.C. Potters from New Mexico Pueblos were guests of President and Mrs. Richard Nixon at the White House in the 1970's. At a reception at the White House, potters from each pueblo presented an example of their traditional pottery to Mrs. Nixon. My mother was the oldest of the group. During our visit we went to the Smithsonian Institution where we saw many different pots from many different places. It was such a wonderful sight to see! My mother's pottery, along with the other potters', was to become a permanent collection at the Smithsonian Institution. It was then, in my later life, that I became interested in making pottery and have been making and selling traditional pottery ever since. Before I started making pottery I used to only help create the designs for my mother, but I did not work with the clay to make the pots. She would make the pots and I would watch.

My mother was Santana Melchor; she was the matriarch of a family of potters, and she was my teacher. She learned pottery making from her mother, and her mother learned it from her mother. The skill is handed down from the family; the family has been making pottery a long time. Pots are formed with coils of our clay, then decorated with natural dyes and fired in pits. Some designs include flowers, geometric designs, and birds.

Many years ago she used to sell them at the Portal of the Governors in Santa Fe.

The gourd and rock that I use today to smooth the pots were the same ones used by my mother. The rock is over 100 years old. I get my clay from the Santo Domingo Pueblo hills. To make the clay I mix the sand and clay together until it is right. After it is all mixed, I start making pottery. After the pottery is made, they are put in the sun to dry. After they get dry, I paint them white or red, and then I put designs on them. I make my own paint from the bee weed plant. I use the 100 year old rock that was once my mother's to polish the pottery. I use the yucca brush for my paint brush, just like the old ways. After I put all the designs on the pot, I start firing them. My designs are flowers, leaves, birds, and other designs and they all have special meanings. You have to have a full mind when you are making the pots. Your mind can't be wandering. The clay knows when you do not have a full mind because the pot will not take form into shapes. The same with the firing, you have to put your full mind into making the fire, so the fire is good, and then the designs on the pots will come out clear. Each time you learn. Prayers are important.

A challenge for me sometimes is during the firing of the pottery. If the firing is too hot, or not hot enough, it will hurt the pottery. Firing has to be on a clear day when the ground is dry. Otherwise, the pots will turn black or break, and our pottery cannot be sold at market. Then we have to start all over again and that takes a lot of time. Getting ready for the Santa Fe Market takes months of preparation which is why I begin 4 to 5 months before the event.

Teaching all of my children is very important to me and the village. All of my children learn some part of the business. They start with small pots until they feel confident. Some are afraid to handle the clay. The children are interested because they have learned that the money they make can buy their school clothes and supplies. We all work together and depend on each other. This is how we live and work.

Keeping this part of my culture of pottery making is important for many reasons, it is also the way we make our money for groceries and clothing, and it helps us to be able to send our children to private high school and to college. Many years ago we used to trade our pottery for necessary items, like food, water, cooking supplies, clothing, and fire wood. People from all over would come to the village to get our pottery.

When we are at market, people sometimes ask to buy the pottery for less than it is marked. We have to help them understand all the time and work it takes to make the pottery. We tell our stories so they understand why we make our pottery. We come to an agreement when people want to deal—we need the money, they want the pot. We think about the many hours it took to make the pottery and we want to get our hard work back and to make money. Buyers come to the house after they read about us in the books or on the internet.

Crucita Melchor

TRIBE: Santo Domingo Pueblo

EDITOR'S NOTES: Crucita Melchor has the entrepreneurial characteristics it takes to have a successful business: She has ambition—always prepared for opportunities that come her way and knowledge, for she has a notebook of wisdom in her mind that she is passing on to the next generation. Crucita creates conversations with her customers when selling her projects so they understand value. Her loyal customers return each year to buy more of her work. She also teaches her skill to her children when they are ready to learn and encourages all family members to have ownership in the product. Crucita's company, Pottery by the Melchors, is located in Santo Domingo Pubelo, New Mexico.

Look for healing in the right places—in people who love you and positively support you physically and emotionally.

—*Laralyn RiverWind*

Beauty (Care Products) from Ashes

Laralyn RiverWind—Research shows that successful people start and stop over and over. They work at, or start, an average of twelve businesses before finally finding their niche. Such is the case with my career—and my life.

My life has been a series of such starts and stops, both personally and professionally. But through each start and stop, I gained knowledge and experience. My life is not typical—I have been stalked, raped, and nearly killed. When I was but 16, living with my missionary parents in the Marshall Islands, I was nearly murdered. My escape was nothing short of a miracle. My parents rescued me from my would-be murderer, breaking his ribs in the process. Even after his arrest, this man strangled and almost killed the jailer. I later learned that my attacker had killed twelve other people, and I was the first to escape with my life. I took comfort in the arms of my Creator, whom I knew had a plan for my life. I was still alive and I was determined to begin again.

A new start came briefly when I returned to the States for college. I quickly gained knowledge, academically and socially. However, one thing I had yet to learn was how to NOT be a victim. A date rape by my boyfriend took my virginity, and I felt so ashamed, blaming myself and remaining in what became an abusive situation for over a year, trying to right what was wrong. When I became pregnant, my abusive partner insisted that I get an abortion, threatening to kill me if I did not comply. When I refused, he tried to run me over with his car. It was then that I knew I needed to stop going down this destructive path and seek a new beginning. I did so in the middle of the night, escaping with just one suitcase, my mother driving the getaway car. She drove well over a thousand miles without sleeping that night or the following day. Fearing his repeated threats to hunt me down and kill me if I left, I went into hiding, abandoning college scholarships in favor of creating a safe environment for my unborn child.

I hid for years with my baby boy, always looking behind me, wondering when I would be caught and killed, or when my son might be kidnapped. For too many years I slept with a suitcase under my bed, packed with clothes and as much cash as I could spare, in case I had to run again.

Living with family half a country away from home, I gradually found refuge from the terror of my small world, and a new world opened to me. With the help of Creator, I survived physically and emotionally. I can speak openly now because I am healed from my past. I gained healing through spiritual encounters and a support system of family and friends. For those of you who find yourself in this situation, know that prayer is your best weapon to fight off fear and apathy. Seek support and know when to get out of any degrading or dangerous situation. While it doesn't always seem so, you are not alone! To get truly free, you must consciously decide not to carry the sickness of the past with you. You must take the good medicine of support, forgiveness, and love, and start again to make your own future.

There have been starts and stops in my professional journey as well. My father taught me herbal medicine as a child, so I turned that interest into a Bachelor's Degree in Biology, working on it even through pregnancy, hospitalizations, and child rearing. I took on a number of business endeavors to supplement my income while I worked on my degree. Mary Kay Cosmetics was one such business that helped me understand skin care products, as well as taxes and business law. Once my degree was completed, I entered medical school, and while the first year was good background for my future, I left for several reasons. One reason was that medical school conflicted with my cultural values. In Western culture, medicine seems mostly concerned with getting a person through whatever health crisis he or she is in at the time. It is less about good medicine—keeping a person well and whole.

But the main reason I left medical school was because my children needed me. It was at this time that I discovered that my children were being abused while I was in school. My support system was gone and now my children had become victims. While I had gained personal strength and knew that I would never be victimized again, I did not see this coming with my children. I refused to let this pattern of abuse repeat itself.

So a new journey began. I took a job at a national body care chain, which turned my attention to skin, skin, and more skin. Having suffered all of my life from a genetic skin condition with no relief from market products or even prescriptions, I returned to the herbal remedies that I had learned from my father so many years earlier. During my hospital and medical school years, my skin suffered from frequent hand washing and harsh chemicals, so I developed a salve to heal my dry, cracked hands. It wasn't until I returned to my roots that I began to understand myself and started to discover what I loved and what niche I could fill. I researched and developed herbal products, at first just for myself and family. But friends in need of skin rescue used these products and began to encourage me to market them. I knew what made good body care products and how to sell them. Between 2002 and 2008, I concentrated on developing my herbal care products, testing them at Pow-Wows to get important feedback for customers' needs and wants.

With this new start, I have found my niche. Native Touch is now three years old. It is growing despite recession challenges. In the past year, we have seen a 400% increase over our last fiscal year, and we have expanded our product line.

I continue to see value in education and learning on all levels. My educational interests are integrally linked to my business. Now that I am in a healthy marriage with children nearly grown, I am back in school, working on becoming a Doctor of Naturopathy. Naturopathy concentrates on allowing the body to maintain a balance of health, recovering naturally from injury, illness, and other environmental challenges. I am learning more about good medicine for the physical body, studying ways to allow the body to heal itself by determining what needs replenishing—vitamins, healthy foods, proper nutrients, more rest, additional activity. This degree will advance my knowledge of herbs so that I can develop more natural body care products and improve client care.

Good medicine for the soul is also a part of my focus. My husband and I work with Natives to encourage cultural expressions of worship rather than conforming to European forms. Through this ministry, we share that Yeshua ("Jesus" in Hebrew) did not dictate a certain way of worshipping, and that using drums, flutes, and dance movement is glorifying to God, not evil as some believe. We teach Biblical reconciliation, forgiveness, and healing while retaining our tribal identity. Our band, The Blessed Blend, spreads wellness and wholeness through music.

Personal healing and forgiveness were important for me to overcome my abusive past. So, too, are they necessary for Native people. Generations of victimization, neglect, and abuse have negatively impacted Native people for too long. While we have a right to suffer in the hurt of the past, we can choose, instead, to experience a better life than what our abusers have dictated for us. With a determination to forgive and overcome the wrongs of the past, we are able to heal and then focus on making a brighter, successful future.

Good medicine brings healing, both to the body and to the spirit. You must look for healing in the right places—in people who love you and positively support you physically and emotionally. It may be just one or two people, but do not forget that you can also turn to your tribe as an entity. With encouraging people and God's help, you can achieve your vision and give birth to your creation. While it is true that birth is hard work and brings pain, do not let that stop you, for with that pain comes healthy new life.

Laralyn RiverWind

TRIBE: Cherokee, Muskogee Creek, Irish & Scottish

EDITOR'S NOTES: Laralyn RiverWind is busy all the time! In addition to her business and schooling, she cares for her two children. Her band, The Blessed Blend, combines Native American and Celtic music, incorporating the harp, flutes, bagpipes, Native and Celtic drums, and vocals. The group has three CD's, the first of which was nominated for several "NAMMYs" (Native American Music Award) and is currently providing music for a film soundtrack. Her other interests include falconry, pottery, pine-needle basketry, cornhusk doll making, biking, painting, and weaponry. Her vision is to continue to provide "good medicine" to others.

Chapter Six

Serving Others

Give people something truly substantial to hold onto.

—*Kay Oxendine*

Something Substantial to Hold Onto

Kay Oxendine—People still like to hold onto something substantial. How true, in so many ways! Like newspapers everywhere, the newspaper that I edit and publish, *360 View*, is in stiff competition with the internet as a news source. And yet I hear from my readers that many of them still like to hold "something substantial" in their hands. While most newspapers focus on the problems of a community, the goal of my paper is to illuminate the good being accomplished by everyday citizens. I believe that by telling stories of the best things happening in the area, I can help bring about many positive changes. So we offer our readers "something substantial" to hold onto—encouragement and an uplifting experience.

I wrote my first book in the fifth grade as a class assignment. I wrote about my family, the community in which I lived, and special events that I remembered or was told, like my parents meeting and "having to get married," or my grandfather, Joseph Richardson, the first Native Boy Scout leader in North Carolina, drowning before my father' eyes.

Even after all of these years, my mother kept this book for me. I still have this book and show it to people as an inspirational tool to "follow your dream." My mother has always been my inspiration and biggest fan.

My local community got me started in this publishing endeavor. I started as editor for *The Country Courier*, in Virginia, and about one month after that job ended, I was asked to edit a small newspaper that covered a broader area. When the publisher decided to close that paper, the community again stepped forward and offered to help me get my own paper up and running.

There are several newspapers that cover surrounding counties and have a variety of readers. However, my community was seeking a newspaper that connected all of these communities. This has proven to be a great marketing tool and highly successful because we find that folks want to know what's happening to their neighbors in the next county.

Since we are a small newspaper, a few people do many jobs. My readership is about sixteen thousand, but because it is published online, potentially it can be seen by millions. I do much of the work myself, gathering stories with the help of neighbors, friends, and community members. I often see the process from start to finish. After I track down a story, I interview, take pictures, write, do the layouts and graphic arts, work with the advertising sales team, and then coordinate the delivery. We are building our own carrier force for delivery, which is proving to be both efficient and effective.

Many topics of interest are typical of small towns—local sports, local government, local schools, parks and special activities in the community. However, my paper never leaves without a story related to an American Indian topic. These stories deal with the progressiveness of the American Indians. I write about the artisans, the push for federal recognition, and the annual Pow-Wows. I especially focus on the good news within our communities and always draw attention to smaller businesses. When I write, I have to keep in mind the diversity of my readers, which include African Americans, Caucasians, Native Americans, and Hispanic people, as well as rural communities.

My stories focus on the positive. For example, in a recent issue, the front page story was about a woman who willingly underwent bone marrow surgery because she matched a recipient. Another story spoke of a woman who desired to educate children using her horses, while yet another focused on a young African American preacher who is making a difference in his community.

With the U.S. economy wavering, selling the paper right now is difficult. Even with the difficult times, I felt that it was a good time to start a business to serve the needs of the community in which I live. In some ways, it is an even better time to get involved with news and information. I believe positive news can heal a community that is struggling. People need a source of real news—good news now more than ever. A good newspaper is central to the growth and success of any community. I am pleased that we are currently on our 26th bi-weekly issue, on the cusp of our 2nd year of publication—an accomplishment of which I am proud!

One challenge I face regularly is being able to get funding to supplement the paper. We sell advertisements as revenue, but as I mentioned, with the current economy, not all businesses can afford advertising. Because we feel that together we can survive these tough times, we are willing to work with businesses so that everyone benefits.

People often falsely assume that because I have an American Indian-owned business, money just "falls from the sky." Many folks think that, due to my heritage, I can just "get" money from the government, the casino, or small minority business grants. But that is not the case. As with every other business venture, financial reward comes with hard work and long hours. Some days it is only my spirituality that helps me get through. I know that I have a great product and I believe in what I do, so I persevere.

Have you ever heard the term "Crab or Cricket Theory"? It happens especially in the Indian communities, where a person is judged poorly when she begins to climb the ladder of success. Some in a community conclude that a person is not worthy of making it as a Native American. Even though this has happened to me, I don't allow this theory to hinder my progress in any way. I realize that the best thing to do is prove to our communities that we can be successful in business—both as women and American Indians. It is important to show the youth that we can do well personally and continue to do good for our communities.

Through my own difficulties, including a painful divorce, I have learned to rely on my inner strength and the strength gained from the "broken backs" of so many ancestors who have gone before. As the mother of two children myself, I have come to realize that the real heroes in my life have been women like my mother, my aunties, and my grandmothers. In this list I must include my extended pow-wow family, who have always helped me "climb back up." This family, plus my own stubbornness, helped me emerge stronger, smarter, and more determined.

Publishing a newspaper is hard work. It means long hours with little pay. But I believe that I was led to do a good thing, and the right thing. I am giving people something truly substantial to hold onto.

Kay Oxendine

TRIBE: Haliwa-Saponi Tribe

FAVORITE BOOK: *The Bible*

SOCIAL MEDIA: FACEBOOK: Kay Oxendine
LINKEDIN: pub/kay-oxendine TWITTER: akayo62

WEBSITE: www.360view.us

EDITOR'S NOTES: Kay Oxendine is the Editor and Owner of 360 View Newspaper in Richmond, Virginia. She studied Mass Communication/Public Relations at the University of North Carolina at Pembroke. Kay is a strong Native American woman who loves life. She is a single mom, who adores her babies Rachel and Johnathan and feels blessed everyday that God brought them to her.

Part of my success is participating and living my culture and heritage and embracing my tribal traditions.

—Karen Yeahquo

Time To Be Whole

Karen Yeahquo—It took an illness to make me whole. It was through serious trials that I found my true self and reaffirmed my spirituality.

I was the oldest girl of nine children. I was handed much responsibility early as I helped in my parents' home—a place abundant with children and money worries. From that came a determination to bring in extra income, as well as the determination to make it on my own. My great-grandmother wore traditional Cheyenne attire, so I naturally absorbed the patterns and colors of the tribe. I began by beading, taught to me by my mother and grandmother. In my 20's my skills were good enough that I was able to re-create one of my great-grandmother's dresses, using vintage material and beads from as far away as Czechoslovakia. Eventually I made garments for family members, but since I was employed, often working ten hours a day, I didn't have much time to devote. Most of my beading was done just for relaxation and enjoyment. When possible, I took advantage of tribal ceremonies and events to observe and study traditional attire. I remember thinking, as most people do, that if I didn't have to work eight hours a day, I would have the time to do what I really love.

That time was given to me in the form of breast cancer.

I was 39 years old when I underwent chemotherapy and radiation. While the prognosis was good for the cancer, the therapy took its toll. The chemotherapy damaged my liver to such extent that I was now in need of a transplant. I spent 6-7 years of my life in and out of the hospital and was forced, after twenty-five years of working, to take disability. It was during this time that I reflected and prayed, recalling my Indian roots and traditions. Perhaps it was a near-death experience, or a dream, or some kind of a trace—call it what you will—but I traveled back to that era of the traditional, and I saw past generations and felt God's presence like never before. Even though my body was not healing, my spirit was.

I lost ten years of my life to illness. I had to be cancer-free for three years before I could even be put on the waiting list for a liver. When I finally got one, the process of full recuperation took five more years. Through all of this I had my deepest walks with God and I never once thought about dying. I believed—and still do—that I had been sent to help others, and that I was still needed to help somebody else when I got well. And now, I had been given the time!

My work is about making traditional Native dress using authentic colors and designs. But I do not limit my work to one tribe. Mostly my clientele are my own Cheyenne and Kiowa people, plus Comanches and other Plains people. I design for men and women, as well as children. I research to learn their colors, patterns, and designs as well. It is through the colors and patterns that a tribe is recognized. The people who come to me are seeking their identity. They want to be recognized and acknowledged for who they are. They want to glance into the past and remember their heritage. My garments give them that. Many come to me and we talk about their memories and look at photographs. From this information, and from my own research, I create designs and patterns from within, working as the spirit guides. These traditional beaded pieces help people learn their identity, showing them who they are and filling in their background. During the two weeks that it takes to make a piece, it is as if the garment begins to create itself. I am merely the hands for it. Each shawl, or dress, or breast plate carries a piece of my spirit with it.

I believe that it is through my work that I help others find their authenticity. Traditions of the tribes are not necessarily lost, but they are held onto tightly because they are so precious. Because of this, I am careful to create only for those who recognize and value the story behind a piece of work. It is important that both the buyer and I see that meaning and understand the true worth. While some would argue that a piece is expensive, others understand that it is not just art that I share, but a way of life.

The gift that I have been given allows me to create and live in my traditions. For that I am grateful. Because I have been given so much—including time—I like to gift my creations to those who can' t afford them. Sometimes I even help those less fortunate by having them create with me to gain an appreciation for this way of living. When I struggle with my work because I can't focus or the needle breaks, I am reminded of words from our Creator, "Come to me" (Matt. 11:28-30) and I am set back on the productive path.

There are many forms of success. To be successful on any level, the risk is taking the first steps and changing—not just settling for what you have. As a Native American with health issues, I have had to go to greater lengths than most and I possess a strong will to succeed. A person can choose to either be discouraged and defeated by failure or to learn from it. A successful person always has many projects and looks forward to each of them. Part of my success is participating and living my culture and heritage and embracing my tribal traditions.

Everything that I am, dream to be, or hope to do are because of my Heavenly Father. Ah Ho, Ma 'heo'o.

Karen Yeahquo

TRIBE: Cheyenne and Kiowa

EDITOR'S NOTES: Karen Yeahquo won 2nd Place at Red Earth Art Show in 2008 with a Traditional Cheyenne child's shell dress. In addition to her business, TwoStrikes Creations in Carnegie, Oklahoma, Karen is researching the forgotten soldiers in the US Army, the Cheyenne and Arapaho Indian scouts. Her plan is to bring their stories to light through family interviews and the designing of the military jackets worn between 1865 and 1942.

Karen also gives back by participating in various elementary classes designed around arts and crafts, storytelling, and Native songs and dancing, where she emphasizes education plus traditions. These activities promote the preservation of tribal customs and traditions.

Having an entrepreneurial spirit is having the wisdom to be patient while persevering to achieve goals, and knowing when to lead and when to follow.

—Rose W. Robinson

The Power of Sharing Knowledge

Rose W. Robinson—Rose Robinson loved mentoring others and she vowed she would share her knowledge with anyone who would listen. She believed knowledge was empowerment, and that "empowerment" was the key to success. She came of age in the late 1960's and 1970's at the height of Native American activism in Washington, D.C. and used her creativity and passion to help Native people at the national and local level. She freely shared her knowledge and contacts, was an advocate for Native women's issues, and encouraged, mentored, and assisted Native Americans nationwide in achieving their policy, business, and personal goals.

During her early professional career in Washington, D.C., while working as a public information officer in the Office of the Commissioner for Indian Affairs, Rose noticed the need for greater news and information in tribal communities. Inspired by those starting or managing Native American newspapers, she left federal service to become the first female Executive Director of the American Indian Press Association (AIPA). Modeled after the Associated Press, Rose oversaw a weekly news feed to dozens of tribal newspapers across the country with the goal of creating an informed citizenry about activities in Washington affecting Indian Country.

Whether running a small non-profit, a consulting business, or a Native American program for a large foundation, our mother understood that a successful entrepreneur needs to produce income to sustain any endeavor. In the beginning, however, it can be challenging. Whether seeking grants from foundations or building a client base, one must be creative, marketable, and prepared with a strong business plan. Entrepreneurs must have revenue projections and an understanding of the mission and vision of the organization. Rose understood that it takes a lot of grit and determination to succeed.

Rose was born on the Hopi reservation in Arizona. While a small child, she moved with her family to Nevada. After high school, she attended Haskell Indian Institute, a Bureau of Indian Affairs boarding school in Kansas, where she received a certificate in commercial arts in 1951. At that time there were very few career choices open to female students—mostly careers in nursing, teaching, domestics, or secretarial. She chose the latter, and, in 1951, landed an administrative support position with the BIA in Aberdeen, South Dakota. After her first year there, she had an opportunity to go to Washington, D.C. and work at the headquarters of the Bureau of Indian Affairs. In those days, the BIA was one of the few places an American Indian woman could get a job in federal government. She jumped at the opportunity, knowing it would change her life. There she met other American Indian women from across the country. The experience allowed her to look beyond the traditional Hopi ways and rural life and to experience the world in a broader sense.

When Rose arrived in D.C., she was fascinated by how the city was a crossroads for people from across Indian

Country and around the world. She spent time learning about different tribes, their cultures, language, and history, and she was energized by her new surroundings. In the big city, Rose was a social butterfly; she loved life, loved learning, and had a natural curiosity about people.

Rose left an impression on those she encountered. Her strong writing skills guided her in the direction of journalism. In the early 60's, our mother left the BIA to become writer and editor of *Smoke Signals*, a publication of the Indian Arts and Crafts Board at the U.S. Department of the Interior. After that, she worked for the Office of the Commissioner of Indian Affairs, which inspired her to take on the role of Executive Director at AIPA. While there, she mentored a number of women who were running tribal newspapers and worked to develop aspiring American Indian journalists. Late in the '70's Rose started the Native American Program for the Phelps-Stokes Fund. It was here that her entrepreneurial spirit soared. She produced and published *The Exchange*, sharing her knowledge of philanthropic organizations to help other American Indians gain access to foundation funding. Mom built bridges between major foundations in New York City and countless tribes and tribal organizations, particularly tribal colleges. During this time, she co-founded the American Indian College Fund and served on the boards of the American Indian Graduate Center and the National Indian Education Association.

Although our mother's life seemed glamorous, it was not always that way. During those Washington, D. C. years,

Rose married and had a family, but the marriage did not last. Being a single parent was difficult. As the sole bread winner, she had to ensure that the family had the basic necessities, but she was also responsible for holding her family together emotionally. With all of her family in the Southwest, she did not have easy access to a typical support system, so Rose created her own "family" by building a network of female Native American friends. A key pillar of her extended family was the friendships she gained through membership in organizations such as the North American Indian Women's Association and the American Indian Society of Washington.

Rose viewed herself as a broker—not so much of finances but of knowledge. After her work with the Phelps-Stokes Fund, Rose moved to Chicago to run the Native American program for the Evangelical Lutheran Church in America. She continued to share information and mentor others. She helped people write proposals, read and develop budgets, learn to research, and get published. Her experience with fundraising became an asset for her, and she willingly dispensed this knowledge to other American Indian women.

The year 1992 brought about the 500th anniversary of non-tribal celebrations of Columbus' arrival in this country. With it came nationwide organized Native American protests in the form of "500 Years of Resistance." Even though it seemed to go against her Native background, Mom held a different perspective. Rather than protest, she believed that a celebration of the 500 years of survival of Native

American people was a way to help heal the wounds they and their ancestors suffered since 1492, and worked with Indian and non-Indian religious leaders from across the country to design it. Always the bridge-builder, Rose even reached out to the Italian American Foundation to invite them to join in the celebration. The result was an historic service at the National Cathedral in Washington, D.C., that was attended by over 3,000 Native and non-Native celebrants, the former representing indigenous cultures from the Western Hemisphere and beyond. But to us, her family, this celebration was not just about Native American survival after Columbus, it was about the survival—and success—of one rural Native American woman—our mother—in the big city.

Rose always capitalized on her natural curiosity and resourcefulness. Successful people like her know who they are and where they are going. They have constant faith in themselves and others and maintain a positive outlook. Having an entrepreneurial spirit is having the wisdom to be patient while persevering to achieve goals, and knowing when to lead and when to follow. Because of her keen intellect, passion for helping others, and fearlessness, she gained nationwide respect across Indian Country and won awards for her achievements. While she is no longer with us, we recognize our mother's legacy of bridge building, voluntarism, and empowerment in our lives and in the lives of those she touched.

Rose W. Robinson

TRIBE: Hopi

FAVORITE QUOTE: *When life hands you lemons, make lemonade* and *Knowledge is Power.*

EDITOR'S NOTES: This story was told from the perspective of Roanne Shaddox and her sister, Robin Robinson Shield about their Mom, Rose W. Robinson. Rose operated her entrepreneurial ventures under the name of RRS Associates. She was a strong believer in the value of voluntarism. Rose served on numerous non-profit boards and committees in the areas of philanthropy and service including the American Indian Graduate Center, the American Indian College Fund (which she co-founded), the Council on Foundations' Advisory Committee on Pluralism in Philanthropy, the American Red Cross' Indian Program Advisory Committee, the Episcopal Church USA's Economic Justice Implementation Committee, the National Indian Lutheran Board, Church Women United Executive Council, the North American Indian Women's Association, the National Indian Education Association, the National Capital Girl Scouts Council, and others.

Surrounding ourselves with such gifted people has caused us to always seek to attain a higher artistic level in our own work.

—Ellie and Elvira Hesse

We Watched and We Learned To "Just Do the Right Thing"

Ellie and Elvira Hesse—She always wore an apron. That apron was a part of who our mother was—a keeper of hearth and home. She passed away when we were very young and our memories don't go much beyond that tangible piece of cloth—often used to wipe our noses, shoo us from the kitchen and occasionally as a hiding place. Perhaps it is this piece of fabric, after all these years, that has inspired our love of sewing.

The duties of our mother now fell to our father. Our father is the heart of where our story lies. He was a blessing for his twelve motherless children. It was our mother's dying wish that our family stay together. This was not an easy accomplishment, but our father honored her wish, utilizing the kindness of friends and neighbors to help with the children. When the county tried to step in to take the children, my father refused. The older siblings alternated each day staying home from school to care for the five preschoolers, trying to stay out of the suspicious eye of the school authorities. How our father was able to keep us together and care for us after Mother's death is still a source of wonder and amazement. Dad worked two jobs most of his life. In addition, he cooked, cut our hair, mended, and even sewed our clothes.

We children helped as we could, working in the onion fields—weeding row by row, then later harvesting the onions, tossing the yellow orbs into gunnysacks. Other odd jobs included mowing in the summer and raking in the fall. The money we made was used to buy our one pair of shoes and school clothes for the upcoming year. Our large vegetable garden supplemented our grocery budget. Dad was a good cook, but our meals were simple—tortillas and beans or tortillas and fried potatoes. No matter how little we had, Dad always found another place at the table for anyone in need. He showed by example his unspoken mantra, "Just do the right thing." We watched, and we learned.

But there was another side of my father, his artistic side. It is unclear how he found time or energy, but Dad taught himself to oil paint and to speak Greek. He did woodcarving, making many of our home furnishings. He even built a bed with drawers for my sister and me. One playful example of his creative talent was the giant snow bunny that he made in the yard, right next to the county road. It was huge and got a lot of attention, even being written about in the local newspaper.

No doubt this is where we draw our inspiration and talent for sewing. But the actual lessons have come from our mother-in-law. Again, we watched, and we learned. As young married women (two of us sisters married her two sons), we took instruction from her, guided with encouragement and patience as we pursued a sometimes frustrating endeavor. Our love of sewing led to quilting, also taught by our mother-in-law. Her ability to juxtapose colors and create unique patterns helps us to strive to improve our own level of work. We draw further inspiration from being acutely aware of our surroundings, especially the changing colors of nature and wildlife.

It was a natural transition, then, to go from quilting for pleasure to quilting for profit. A friend who owns a home used as a retreat center on eighty acres is supporting and encouraging local Wisconsin artisans, and she plans to display and sell our quilts, table runners, and wall hangings. Her guests come from all over the country, giving us a large base of potential customers. She has also agreed to post our quilts on her website, giving us even more exposure nationwide.

Our products include all varieties of quilts, and also table runners, wall hangings, lap robes, and of course, aprons not unlike the ones our mother used to wear. Currently our business comes mostly through word of mouth and local connections—shows, gatherings, and events that showcase our products and ideas. These connections have led us to other artistic women whose creations and talents seem endless. Surrounding ourselves with such gifted people has caused us to always seek to attain a higher artistic level in our own work.

Running a business as a team requires interests and goals that mesh well together. We must be able to make decisions that we both agree upon, and our view for the future of our company must be in sync. It is important that we manage our investments and savings wisely. While others may struggle in a business partnership and view it as a detriment, as sisters, we believe that being able to work as a team is a real asset. We love what we do and it shows in our work.

The "right thing" for our father was to take care of his family, work hard, and always seek to learn. He continued to grow in his own knowledge, and he both inspired and encouraged us to do the same. He believed in education and saw to it that we stayed in school. He taught us that hard work is nothing to be afraid of. From watching his example, we learned these truths that are worth passing on to the next generation: Work hard but take the time to nurture your passion. Live within your means, and discipline yourself to save and invest your money so you can help those in need, as well as be prepared for the future. In business especially, you must be strong and resolute—share your emotions only in private. When you experience prejudice—towards yourself or others—stand up to those who perpetuate it.

Quilting is one way for us to "just do the right thing." Through our work, we share with friends, family, and anyone in need. For example, through our local quilting guild, we became aware of a man who wanted to preserve his mother's memory by having her dresses made into a quilt. We took on this project to help him keep his memories alive. We see our sewing as an opportunity to put a smile on someone's face or give some comfort. It is also one of the best ways we know to honor both our father and our mother.

Ellie and Elvira Hesse

TRIBE: American Indian and Hispanic Descent

FAVORITE QUOTE: *Do what you can with what you have, where you are.* —*Teddy Roosevelt*

EDITOR'S NOTES: Ellie and Elvira Hesse are sisters residing in Montello, Wisconsin. They work from their homes nestled in a pine forest. As co-owners of Fabric Works in the Pines they create quilts featuring natural motifs.

Because they are sisters and were raised with the same values, management and investment decisions for their company come with ease. They are easily able to make decisions as a team.

Ellie and Elvira share a vision of the future of Fabric Work in the Pines and attribute their great working relationship to their lifetime of common experiences.

Once you are able to speak from a spiritual place where you call on your ancestors for guidance, you are able to present new ways of thinking.

—Stephanie Kettler

Hope Nation

Stephanie Kettler—In the summer of 2005, I was introduced to a group of women who were dedicated to providing summer camps for Native children in and around the Navajo reservation. After spending one week each summer with a small community just outside Window Rock, AZ, I learned the importance that culture plays in Native communities and the significance it can have on the health and well-being of our people. This organization was called Field of Plenty.

Field of Plenty's mission was to provide summer camp opportunities for American Indian children and their communities. Working with this non-profit during my personal time, I was able to learn more about who I am as a strong Lakota woman. My people, the Oglala Lakota, are from Pine Ridge, South Dakota but I was raised in an urban area. Living away from Pine Ridge, I endured many things as a young child as a result of the relocation, separation and historical trauma that impacted my family. Living in an orphanage, growing up in foster care, born to alcoholic parents and enduring a dysfunctional family life, I was separated from my culture and therefore, my identity. As many Native people will tell you, there is an innate calling in our blood that screams to us, "reconnect, reconnect!" I have come to believe through my own experience that this calling was an answer to the pain, shame and anger I had experienced about being Native throughout my young life. This calling, in essence, moved me back to the circle, my tribe, and my community. Joining Field of Plenty allowed me to "come back home" in a sense and allowed me the opportunity to give back to my people.

At the same time, I began a new job as a program manager for an American Indian Studies program at a prominent university. This increased my persistence and drive which, I realize now, gave me the chance to surround myself with other Natives and/or like minded individuals. Since the program was housed in a school of Social Work, I was introduced to a larger scale view of all the issues facing Indian Country. In addition, I was able to form relationships, friendships and collaborations with Native people from all over the United States, thus strengthening my position to help carry out the mission of Field of Plenty.

Field of Plenty's mission was born out of a group of non-Native women with loving hearts and compassionate minds. I was the only Native board member of this national organization. Being Native, they were elated to have my perspective and insight. As I watched the planning of camps in Arizona and Missouri, it was hard for me to see something being created in Native communities that did not involve the people from the beginning. This pushed me to speak up and educate the organizers and founder of Field of Plenty about the importance of having the community plan and create their own camps.

Through my work with these youth at summer camps, I saw the huge commitment that Native family and community members had for their children. I listened to the people tell me about Native artists, athletes and spiritual leaders that lived right in their own community. This lead to my request to the board that we provide culturally based youth development opportunities by hiring local artisans from the community to teach their culture. For example, the Navajo artists in Arizona were weavers, singers, medicine men, or potters. Most of the time, I was met with support and agreement. However, there were times that I had to pray for guidance in order to educate the board on how to be culturally appropriate and understanding of the ways of our communities. This was difficult at times but having that strong support system of Native colleagues and friends was very beneficial. I also did a literature search for information written by Native people in the same situation. Although I was able to find a few articles that were helpful, there wasn't much written by Natives concerning their experience. I soon realized that I am of a small percentage of Native women who are embarking on entrepreneurship and leadership in the non-profit sector.

This came with mixed feelings of insecurity and a sense of a lack of empowerment. I knew I had to present my concerns to the founding committee members, which put me at risk of not being heard or understood; I feared it could even mean elimination from the Board of Directors of Field of Plenty. Once I was able to speak from a spiritual place where I call on my ancestors for guidance, I was able to present new ways of thinking and teach them from a holistic perspective rather than the linear viewpoint they had learned from their limited education of Native people.

These new concepts lead to tremendous changes within the organization. At our annual board meeting in 2008 I was voted in as President of the Board. As board members' terms were up and others resigned, they were replaced with Native people. With five of the seven board members Native, we had a renewed sense of direction and momentum.

Unfortunately, the camps and the re-development of the non-profit took a turn when my sister passed away suddenly. My momentum and the momentum and growth of Field of Plenty came to a halt. Her passing was due to many issues that Natives continue to face every day. Her loss was so unexpected that it was difficult for me to stay working in Indian Country without being reminded of who she was and why she wasn't with us anymore. The grief took over and for this past year, I put Field of Plenty aside.

Even throughout the year of healing, the non-profit was always burning in my heart. As I prayed for direction on how to come to terms with my sister's loss, I was constantly reminded of what I could have done to help her; what her community could have done to help her. It came back to pride. My sister suffered from low self-esteem, disempowerment, and shame. I truly believe that if she knew in her heart what it meant to be a Lakota woman, if she reconnected and learned the ways of our people, she would have been stronger and it's quite possible that her life could have been saved. I will never know if that's true but I do know what it meant for me to learn where I came from and to surround myself with proud, positive, strong Natives.

Through the loss of my sister and the healing process, a new momentum has been created in my heart. I have decided to change the name of Field of Plenty to Hope Nation, pending a vote by the board. A new, stronger focus on pride and hope has been created. Through my network of connections at the university as well as the Native leaders I have come to call friends across the country, this non-profit will re-establish itself with a goal to provide several camps in the summer of 2012. Reinstallation of the board, fundraising and organizing at least four strong camps in urban and reservation areas are goals for us this year.

Although Natives continue to be amongst the highest statistical rates for disease, abuse and death, I know now, more than ever, we are a resilient people. These hardships only make us stronger. Respecting and honoring our culture is what will sustain our communities. Knowing our traditional values and applying them in a modern society gives us the ability to preserve our way of life and teach others a new way of thinking.

Stephanie Kettler

TRIBE: Oglala Lakota

FAVORITE BOOK: *Pride and Prejudice* by Jane Austen

FAVORITE QUOTE: *Trust yourself. You know more than you think you do.* —Dr. Spock

WEBSITE: www.fieldofplenty.org

EDITOR'S NOTES: Stephanie Kettler lives in St. Louis with her three children. Hope Nation provides camp experiences for Native children and youth in urban and reservation areas. Through the camps, well-being and self-esteem are enhanced via emphasizing and preserving Native culture, values, and heritages. Children and their families are served in reservations, rural and urban areas across the United States. Local artisans and storytellers keep the culture alive through traditional teachings, arts, theatre, and sports. Hope Nation is dedicated to passing Native history and tradition from one generation to the next by employing members of the Native community. The Native youth are able to see a connection between the preservation of their heritage and their future as Natives.

Chapter Seven

Living the Dream

I am fortunate to have my mother as my mentor. But, no matter where this business takes us, I am most fortunate to simply have a wonderful mother.

—Nicole Wheeler

Mother & Mentor

Nicole Wheeler—Two years ago, when asked to be co-editors of *A Cup of Cappuccino for the Entrepreneur's Sprit: American Indian Women Entrepreneurs' Edition* my mother and I had no idea what this would mean for us. We were being offered projects in addition to our full time jobs. At the time both of us worked for nonprofits, she in leadership for a national scholarship foundation and I in communications for an Indigenous peoples advocacy group. Both of my parents dedicated their professional lives to causes meaningful to our family, and I have always admired my mother's career. She has worked for universities and nonprofits specializing in increasing diversity at the graduate level. My father was a policy maker for American Indian tribes. And I had never seriously considered a career in the private sector.

But with the promise of this book, she and I decided to start our own company. We wanted a way to legitimize all of the work we had been doing in addition to our full time positions. My mother has the credibility to create a successful company and I have the confidence to think I can help.

Our earliest projects included writing proposals and conducting focus groups. She was helping cultural and civic organizations. I was assisting other groups with fundraising and community outreach. But when someone asked us what our company did, we froze.

We both fumbled over our words. I mumbled something about communication and my mother muttered about leadership. The question was paralyzing for us both. We got in the car and realized that it was time for us to define our mission, vision and services.

Articulating our mission and vision was easy. The wonderful thing about working with your mother is that you have the same values. The principals that govern our operations are inherent in our relationship. They are what we believe and how I was raised. We thought it was important to include a values statement because it is so paramount to our relationship and the way we operate and we wanted to convey that to our clients. We believe in strong work ethic and working in culturally diverse environments in a meaningful and respectful manner. Our cultural values guide the vision of Tovar & Wheeler Consulting, LLC.

After an arduous afternoon of brainstorming, the company emerged officially as a consulting group that strives to strengthen organizations' capacities for leadership development through sustainable initiatives. Our list of services was shortened to something concise enough for clients to understand, but broad enough to encompass many different capabilities.

We only take on projects that are a good fit with our values. The projects truly excite us and we are eager to be a part of them. It would be amazing to someday work full-time as a consultant, but right now we are fortunate enough to be able to balance our workload and our day jobs.

She and I are in different parts of the country so we have a lot of phone calls and utilize resources like Skype™ to video conference. Quarterly, we meet to discuss and review financials. And we do our best to keep our work and professional conversations separate.

People often ask, "What it is like to work with your mother?" It's amazing. Our shared values ensure we are on the same page about the direction of our company. It is only about the superficial that we disagree. To date our most delayed decision has been about the business cards. She likes things earth tone and streamlined. And I am insisting my card has neon ruffles, or something along those lines. But, embracing our differences has allowed us to succeed. She listens to my bold ideas and can find ways to streamline them to success. Our networks are different too. She has relationships with established professionals, and I know young people across the country ready and willing to make a difference.

At 25, to say I own my own company is an accomplishment but I know I still have a lot to learn. Together, my mother and I are learning as we go. Learning about business, about our clients and about each other. I am fortunate to have my mother as my mentor. But, no matter where this business takes us, I am most fortunate to simply have a wonderful mother.

Nicole Wheeler

TRIBE: Hispanic and Comanche descent

EDITOR'S NOTES: Nicole Wheeler lives and works in Baltimore, Maryland. She is the co-editor of *A Cup of Cappuccino for the Entrepreneur's Spirit: American Indian Women Entrepreneurs' Edition*, and co-founder of Tovar & Wheeler Consulting, LLC, an organization dedicated to supporting leadership development initiatives.

Call upon that friend or loved one who believes in you, so that when you struggle to believe, they are ready to remind you of what you can be. Big dreams can turn defeat into destiny!

—Bobbie Nell Vigil

Believe and You Will Achieve

Bobbie Nell Vigil—Sometimes we are our own worst enemies. It is easy to be overwhelmed and defeated before you even get started—*I have this idea, but I'm not sure anyone would be interested in it, and I'm not good enough on my own. Where will I find the money for start-up costs? I don't have any real experience or training in this area. How will I get licensing, find vendors, or promote my business?* Admittedly, all of these concerns are legitimate. But the beauty of being your own boss is that you are the only one who sets your limitations. There are no predetermined formulas or rules to follow. Being your own boss means that the possibilities are endless!

When I began to think seriously about starting a restaurant, I didn't know exactly how to go from an idea to a reality. I called the state and inquired about the process for obtaining a business license and the subsequent steps that followed. I found out that I needed to establish a location that would require inspections. I knew I would need a food distributor, kitchen equipment, dining room furniture, and an identifying look, sound, and feel—so it was designed to be comfortable and inviting. My goal was to provide the customer with a space to relax, rejuvenate, and refuel. This is what I envisioned my food establishment to provide—food, drink, and rest. What I wanted to eliminate are the additional concerns that customers sometimes have: Will I be able to be served and eat in the brief time I have? Will the food be hot, delicious, and reasonably priced? Will my needs be attended to quickly? At the Morning Star, the answer is yes! As the chef, my husband Darryl attends to the back of "the house," providing quality food for our customers, while I run the front of the house, providing the quality of service our customers expect and deserve.

So we started with not much more than an idea. We gave up our regular paychecks, so at this point we had no income, no savings, and no clear way to pay our bills and high mortgage. Darryl and I didn't talk about our fears often, but they were there. Everything we had was tied into the success or failure of our new venture, the Morning Star Café. But we believed in the idea, and we believed in each other. His recipes were good, and I was convinced that when people tasted the product, they would become repeat customers. I believed in myself, too; no one was going to do this for me, and in the face of my own fear, I had to have courage—not only for myself, but for Darryl and my children. So we borrowed money from friends and family, and we sold items that we could do without. All the while I kept my eye on the outcome I wanted. I created a plan, and when I didn't know how to do something, I asked someone or researched for information and ideas, knowing that somewhere someone had done this and I could draw from their knowledge and experience.

After months of planning and preparation, we opened the doors of the Morning Star Café. No one came in those first agonizing hours. My stomach churned with panic. What if I was wrong? What if this was a bad idea? No, this was a *good* idea, and if I had to drag people in and feed them for free, I would do it! If I had to put on a gorilla suit and wave people down in the road, then so be it! And then, a car stopped. Two ladies came in and ordered breakfast. They praised the food. And then two more came in, and then more, and more. Word of mouth is a powerful thing, and during that first month there were lines waiting to get in. We worked nonstop and found ourselves exhausted at the end of each day, but we made enough money to place a second food order and to barely cover our first month's expenses. Morning Star Café now flourishes, but every day we are grateful for every customer—we offer each one our very best, for every person counts and deserves a great experience.

My business is located in Dulce, New Mexico, in Rio Arriba County. The population is approximately 3000 people and is predominately Native American. It is the largest community and tribal headquarters of the Jicarilla Apache Reservation. The 6000 or so families residing in and around this area want a nice place to eat and to enjoy good, healthy food. *Shuba-Wah,* which means "morning star," was selected deliberately as the restaurant's name. Through this name, we wanted to connect to the customers at a personal level and show our personality. The message for our customers was that this is a happy environment and a positive way to start each day. In addition, the Morning Star motto, "Serving Northern New Mexico Fusion," came from the idea of combining foods and tastes from the three ethnicities commonly represented in New Mexico—Native American, Hispanic, and Anglo-American.

Dreaming big is important in a new venture, but so is a big dose of reality. You must believe in yourself and have confidence, but you must also recognize what it takes to make a business work. Gathering capital and human resources to finance and physically run the business is important to keep in mind. A business plan is the most important aspect of starting a restaurant, or any business, for it is the road map that will explain who you are and what your business is and where your future lies. Decisions such as your intended location and business hours are just a sampling of the many details that must go into the planning. For example, for the Morning Star Café', I had to decide whether the restaurant would be a formal or informal establishment and where to locate to maximize targeted customers. I had to determine menu items, recipes, hours of operation, and seating capacity. I also had to meet all the regulations of the city and county and get the appropriate licensing.

While I was excited and optimistic, I also had to plan for the very real possibility that I might not have as much business as I had hoped. The "bottom line" is to be able to pay my staff—and myself—because while this is my dream, the reality is that ends must meet.

What will it take for you to achieve your dream? Only you can set your limitations. But just because "reality" can be overwhelming doesn't mean you should give up. Work hard to avoid being your own worst enemy. Put thoughts of doubt out of your head, and keep moving forward one step at a time. With some research and a good plan, you can find success. Call upon that friend or loved one who believes in you, so that when you struggle to believe, they are ready to remind you of what you can be. Big dreams can turn defeat into destiny!

Bobbie Nell Vigil

TRIBE: Jicarilla Apache

FAVORITE QUOTES: *So above, so below, so within, so without. – Emerald Tablet 3000 B.C I am, because we are. –Desmond Tutu*

EDITOR'S NOTES: Bobbie is a mom, a wife, a daughter, an aunt, a runner, horseman, singer, musician, volunteer, artist, an entrepreneur—but mostly, she is whatever she chooses to be – and tomorrow she may be something new.

Have a strong will, take the good and the bad, and always remain positive.

—Rhonda LeValdo-Gayton

Videography with a Vision

Rhonda LeValdo-Gayton—All I wanted to do was run—run in high school, run in college, and run away from any problems I had. I grew up with my grandmother, but as she was getting older, my aunt and uncle took me in. But I always felt different. I worried a lot and running was the only thing that kept me grounded. At Phoenix College in Arizona, I focused on running instead of math and English; consequently, my life course was altered at this point. I was not eligible to continue to run at a four-year school. I was disappointed and had to find a different path. I always wanted to follow in the footsteps of Billy Mills (Oglala Lakota, Sioux), an Olympic gold medal winner and the only American to win the 10,000 meter run. He grew up in poverty and was orphaned at age 12. He turned to sports as a positive force in his life. The early disappointments in our lives led us both toward sports; now I, however, had to face the fact that disappointment would require me to change course and run a different kind of race. Regardless, Billy Mills inspired me to be positive and to think positively.

I decided to attend Haskell Indian Nations University in Lawrence, Kansas. I felt I needed a change, a way to get back on track with my education. This time, I excelled in my classes and started in video production classes, leading me into journalism. Haskell opened to me a diverse world of tribes, students, elders, and native professionals who helped me formulate my professional plan. I then transferred to the University of Kansas (KU) to study broadcast journalism. While there, I delved into radio programming, developing the first Native American produced show. This led to my current program at 90.1 KKFI-FM Kansas City where I have produced "Native Spirit" for the past six years. Multimedia encompasses aspects of graphic design, art, web design, advertising, writing, and photography. This field is very broad, and one can also gain skills in communication. I had a basic overview of applying learned skills to practical projects, such as short video clips and web pages. My degree helped me gain a better understanding of media technology as well as multimedia presentation and artwork. While studying this field, I learned I had to have a basic understanding of all the various aspects of this field to be competitive in the job market.

Returning to work at Haskell after completing my degree, I was relentlessly pushed by a former teacher, Bill Curtis, to pursue a master's degree. Now, even with two children in diapers, and a spouse in another state, I took on the task of teaching while working on another degree. But through all of this, my career benefitted, as I had opportunities to do stories for the Online Newshour (PBS), and I was selected as a semi-finalist by the Pulitzer Center for a contest called "Project Report." Both of these experiences opened the doors for my stories to be viewed by a much larger audience than I anticipated. In 2009, I graduated with my degree. Going to graduate school, which I thought would not be possible, became a reality with perseverance and Billy Mill's message of positive thinking still in my head.

One way to reach out to the American Indian young people is to teach, which I presently do at Haskell Indian Nations

University in Lawrence, Kansas, as an adjunct faculty member. This is a baccalaureate granting university for members of federally recognized Native American tribes in the United States. At this school, I feel that my job is not only to teach but to lead students to discover what they want to do, just like my instructors did for me. Haskell provides a venue for me to teach what I know and love, and it allows me to share my perspective about the need for more American Indians in the field of multimedia. It is important for American Indian people to learn how the media can tell our stories, and it can reach more audiences through today's technology. If I can convince other American Indians to consider this avenue in their career journeys, I know our stories will be told. Unfortunately, my experience in mainstream media is that it does not always provide individuals the opportunities to showcase their talents, and the project focus is narrow and limited. In what is often considered a very creative venue, I found that thinking "outside the box" was not always welcomed.

One day a non-Native producer asked me why he could not get the cooperation of the Native community on a particular story. I informed him it was probably about "trust." The media has portrayed Indian people incorrectly for many years. Native American Indian movies, journalists, and historians have not been kind in the past, especially in the early years of movies and television. Hollywood and news sources still have a long way to go, often portraying Natives in stereotypical ways rather than viewing events through a Native lens. My first-hand experience as an extra in a western confirms this. On the set, those of us playing women and children were portrayed with ragged hair and made up to look dirty and neglected. One upset woman voiced her concerns: "Our women were never dirty or unkempt...you are not portraying us right!"

I am also the current President of the Native American Journalists Association (NAJA). The Native American Journalists Association serves and empowers Native journalists through programs and action designed to enrich journalists and promote Native cultures. I am proud and excited to be a part of a program that wants to improve communications among Native people and between Native Americans and the general public. My goal is to encourage and guide the mainstream society to take our stories and showcase them to the world in a respectful and accurate way.

NAJA is one of four media organizations under the umbrella of Unity: Journalists of Color, Inc. The other members are the Asian American Journalists Association, the National Association of Black Journalists, and the National Association of Hispanic Journalists members. The purpose of Unity is to advocate for fair and accurate news coverage about people of color, and aggressively challenge the industry to staff its organization at all levels to reflect the nation's diversity.

Recently at our annual NAJA conference, our association was the only group that presented a live video webstream of the conference. Many people from the other minority journalism associations were amazed, wondering how a group with little resources could produce such a complex broadcast. We did so because one devoted member, Paul DeMain, of *News from Indian Country* and Indiancountrytv.com, dedicated his time and talents.

My close ties with NAJA and Unity and our kindred purposes often inspire me to create my own business. I envision starting my own Native video production company that would set up and start projects, provide the talent, and develop a 24-hour news feed. Video production would be used at sporting events, schools, plays, weddings, churches, and any other events to provide a means of capturing stories and saving history. In addition, my vision is to create an interactive multimedia system that would provide both non-Native and Native journalists a venue to reach out to American Indian communities and get their stories. This program would allow me to teach ways for the mainstream media to capture our needs and vision accurately. We could then achieve what we are seeking—collaboration rather than contention.

Rhonda LeValdo-Gayton

TRIBE: Pueblo of Acoma

FAVORITE QUOTE: *If you think you'll lose, you've lost; For out in the world we find success begins with a person's will; It's all in a state of mind!* —C.W. Longenecker

EDITOR'S NOTES: Rhonda has two children, Hepanna and Winona, and she is married to Denny Gayton. She is still an avid runner and loves to sew, read, and record videos in her spare time. Rhonda offers these words of wisdom to young people: *Become actively involved in all aspects of your personal finances. Know how to budget. Scrimp—the word I grew up with—wherever and whenever you can. As a leader in any role you take, you should set an example of handling your finances wisely. Have a strong will, take the good and the bad, and always remain positive. Bad things should be viewed as just something to overcome. And always, "Family over everything."*

When you believe in what you do, you don't consider it work.

—Maggie George

A Positive Partnership

Maggie George—Are students learning?

This one question has guided my work for nearly three decades. After spending my career in public institutions, I was tired of dealing with the challenges often associated with universities. I came to a realization that life is too short to be confined by politics and bureaucracy and that my knowledge was too valuable not to be optimized to help students. I took my time, did my research and discovered that I, along with my husband, could fill a niche market.

Realizing that administrators and institutions needed help answering the same question—*Are students learning?* My husband and I founded Indigenous Research Associates in 2002. Our firm strives to help American Indian educators conceptualize, design, implement, and assess school-based programs that promote students' academic achievement and cultivate cultural identities by providing clients state-of-the-art research, evaluation, and strategic planning services.

Our 60 years of combined experience in research and our understanding of Native values help us fill a specialized market. I am a member of the Diné Nation and have my Ph.D. in Higher Education Policy and Leadership from the University of Kansas, a Master's in Guidance and Counseling, and a Bachelor's in Elementary Education from New Mexico Highlands University. My husband, Daniel, is a former program specialist at Diné College and professor in curriculum and critical studies. He earned a doctorate in Educational Foundations. Our unique perspective makes us a perfect fit for work with Tribal Colleges and Native Studies departments at universities.

However, meeting this need has certainly had its challenges. Because our industry is so specialized and largely untapped, determining our market rate base has been difficult. This was our first venture into the private sector and there was a large learning curve regarding the business of our firm. My husband and I are confident in our competency of services, but understanding the ins and outs of business compliances presented us with a new set of challenges.

Most frustrating was understanding the taxation of our company and our services. In 2007 we entered a partnership agreement, which simplified our taxes and gave us greater freedom when outlining responsibilities and benefits. Currently, my husband and I collaborate on the design of a project and then divvy up the deliverables.

We approach our projects holistically and most take a significant amount of time. Contracts last anywhere from two months to five years. It is our hope to build a lasting relationship with our clients that will result in long-term communication for continued progress and evaluation.

Our services include strategic planning, program evaluation, academic assessment, faculty development and academic assessment. As external evaluators, we take our time to get acquainted with our clients and the communities invested in their institution. Quality research is essential to our work and a tenet of our business. Our unique blend of research knowledge and experience in American Indian settings allows us to access community collaboration and critical reflection.

The most common goal that our clients have is to improve scores, rankings, or ratings as they relate to the financial well-being of the university or program. However, the approach of Indigenous Research Associates focuses on improving student success. Clients typically concentrate on accessing funding, but when the long-term goal is shifted from dollars to student success, a more sustainable project is created and the project can achieve success.

It is not enough for administrators only to buy into the project. As researchers, we look beyond the deficit model and "help the poor Indian" attitude. We work to develop plans that make a difference, honor people, and empower people to care about doing the right thing.

We present the research of community needs and strengths as well as student data to the client and then work together to implement a strategy. This is where our unique experiences are key. It is our job to create a plan that fits the mission of an institution founded on a model of Western education while still addressing the needs of a diverse community. It is important for us to demonstrate the values of all parties to create "buy in." To be successful here, the clients must be part of the planning project. When clients work with us to create the project, they understand the goals and how they relate to them personally, professionally and communally. When clients understand the language of the project they become more invested—they care. They understand what part they play and that they are stakeholders. Clients come to realize that we did not hand them a cookie cutter template and that their voices are valued as part of a specialized plan.

We are committed to growth and learning and advocating for these processes within client organizations. When considering a bid, we ask ourselves, "Is this a something we can do? Is this something we care about it?" If we feel a project doesn't directly help students, we opt out. I am an educator and I am passionate about doing the right thing. Because I believe in what I do, I don't consider it work; when I know I'm working for positive student outcomes, I don't really worry about the income. Knowing that students are learning and achieving is reward in itself.

Maggie George

TRIBE: Diné Nation

WEB SITE: www.indigenous-research.org

EDITOR'S NOTES: Maggie George has extensive administrative experience including serving as the Director of the American Indian Program at New Mexico State University, Las Cruces, New Mexico; Director of Educational Equity and Access, New Mexico Higher Education Department, Santa Fe, New Mexico; Academic Vice President, Diné

College, Tsaile, Arizona; and Dean, School of Education, Haskell Indian Nations University, Lawrence, KS. Among many honors received by Dr. George are Recipient of Fulbright-Hays Fellowship - Study of Higher Education in South Africa, Alliance for Equity and Excellence in Minority Serving Institutions and Recipient of Leadership Fellowship for Minority Serving Institutions, Kellogg Foundation and the American Indian Higher Education Consortium. Maggie has served as a volunteer in the Arts, Habitat for Humanity and the Mayor's Task Force for Drug and Alcohol Abuse in Lawrence, Kansas.

Those who are mentored should pay it forward and be mentors to the next generation.

—Margo Gray-Proctor

Indian Oprah: On My Own Terms

Margo Gray-Proctor—Fondly referred to by my professional friends as the *Indian Oprah*, I was born in Pawhuska, Oklahoma, or as I refer to it, the Osage Reservation, where Pawhuska's beginnings can be traced to my people, the Osage Indians.

My parents resembled the couple in the movie *Giant*. Mom was a beautiful woman of grace and class. She was half Osage and half English and French descent. Dad was a full Osage Indian Cowboy. I was the sixth child of seven—also known as *Baby Girl*. Mom and Dad did whatever it took to support the family. I remember my parents always working hard to support our family, for example, when we relocated from Oklahoma to Colorado my Mom worked at a department store while my Dad worked several jobs; one of his jobs was as a cab driver. They had such an entrepreneurial spirit and owned numerous businesses including a dairy farm, bowling alley, cleaning service, and the *White Hair Trading Post*.

It was 1961, we moved from Pawhuska to Arvada, Colorado where I attended Kindergarten through 9th grade. We were the only Native Americans in the suburbs and in our schools. Our parents wanted us to experience the language and culture of both worlds. I excelled in sports as captain of the basketball team, track and field teams and set records in the shot put and played softball throughout the summers.

I was fortunate to have two wonderful parents and six siblings. We were taught to have a great work ethic at a young age and the word 'can't' was not allowed in our vocabulary and if we did use it we received an hour long lecture from my Dad. We moved back to Pawhuska when I was in the 9th grade and I then worked at the trading post throughout my high school years.

I was accepted at Oklahoma State University, but got pregnant during my senior year and had my oldest son Matthew. I decided to attend Northeastern Oklahoma State University because it was smaller and I thought it would be easier for me to take Matthew with me to class; so we attended Northeastern for 2 ½ years. I then made a choice to go into the Indian Police Academy and spent the next 17 years in law enforcement. During this chapter of my life, I experienced many firsts for a Native American woman and as a woman in my law enforcement career. I was the first woman to be a defensive tactics instructor in the State of Oklahoma, CLEET (Council of Law Enforcement and Training Center) and the first Native woman ever to be hired as a Marshal for the Cherokee Nation Marshal Service.

Dad encouraged me to help with Indian law enforcement. If there is a crime committed on Indian land, law enforcement couldn't go on the land. In 1995, I assisted the Osage Nation in setting up a law enforcement department and in the writing the legislation for passage of tribal laws. The last place I worked in the law enforcement area was in Tahlequah, Oklahoma for the Cherokee Nation specializing in sex crimes involving crimes against children. This changed me! I had all I could handle emotionally so when an opportunity came to work in a tribal government position as a legislative aide for the Osage National Council, I took it. Following a 10th Circuit Court decision, I found myself unemployed for the first time. Little did I know, this pink slip would lead me to a greater opportunity and ultimately release the entrepreneurism that was in my family history.

With unemployment checks running out, I knew that I wanted to start my own business working with Tribes. I went to an Engineering Firm's Christmas party with a good friend and met my future business partner Carl Cannizzaro. Carl and I launched Horizon Engineering Services Company in Tulsa, Oklahoma providing professional engineering services to tribes. We are a national company working for tribes across 29 states. The partnership works great with my knowledge of federal and tribal contracting and Carl's civil engineering knowledge.

The economic recession of 2008 presented challenges to most businesses in the nation and we were no exception. We saw the writing on the wall and gathered all employees. Our message was that we were going to do whatever it took and asked our employees to take furlough days in order for everyone to keep their jobs. We all learned some valuable lessons during this recession: focus on core competencies, work hard and always keep in contact with past clients. Relationship building is critical and can make a difference in whether your company succeeds or fails.

It took a few years and a lot of hard work to become profitable, but after thirteen years Horizon Engineering is a multi-million dollar company with 11 employees.

Thinking back, it seems natural that I should be an entrepreneur because I am coming from a family of entrepreneurs including my siblings, parents and grandparents. My first entrepreneurial experience *and* letter from an attorney came as a seven year old. In the back of comic books were order forms for flower and vegetable seeds. I would order seeds and sell them door to door. The money I made from the seeds was invested in candy and I would sell the candy at school for twice the amount it cost me. What I missed is that I was supposed to pay for the seeds after I sold them! When my Dad handed me a letter I had received from the seed companies attorney about not paying for the seeds, my savings and profit margins decreased because my Dad made me send in my money for the seeds that I had sold. To build back my profit margin I responded by expanding my product line with long sticks of bubble gum that I bought for 5 cents each and sold for 10 or 15 cents each. First lesson in business check!

During our teenage years, my younger brother and I worked for our parents at the *White Hair Trading Company* and although I didn't think much about it at the time, I learned many skills including financial (balancing the drawers and making deposits and product inventory), integrity, work ethic and customer service. These skills have served me well in my entrepreneurial ventures. In addition to Horizon, I have owned a spa, a drug testing company and a stained glass business. My theory as an entrepreneur is to always position yourself to sell your company and have your paperwork ready. And . . . never let a failure keep you from starting your next business.

Having a mentor or support system is also important for entrepreneurs. We are often isolated and need to be empowered through the inspiration and wisdom that others can provide. For me, Dave Anderson, founder of Famous Dave's BBQ, was that person. I call Dave the 'Elvis' of BBQ because his employees look at him like they are looking at Elvis. At a time when he really needed to get invigorated about business, Dave drove from Washington D.C. to Oklahoma and spent two days in Tulsa. He told me "You are going to be big—a strong voice for Indian Country. You are the Oprah of Indian Country." I was moved by his words to me. Nobody had made me feel like this. I knew he valued me. Then Dave said to me, "There are some things you need" and we went to Barnes and Noble. While we were there he bought some $500 of business books, audio cds and tapes for me to listen to. He told me he was driving back to Minnesota and handed me the sack of all these things he just bought and told me these are the tools you need. I stood there stunned by this act of genuine generosity. He told me after I was done reading and listening to these "business and life tools" that I needed to pay it forward to someone else. I was fortunate to have an opportunity to stay with Dave and his wife in Minneapolis while he sent me to his "Life Skills Center for Business". These are the types of relationships that are so important to an entrepreneur and those who are mentored should pay it forward and be mentors to the next generation.

The key to achieving success depends on a number of factors including having a strong work ethic, offering personalized service, being fearless and having vision. Horizon competes against national companies with hundreds of employees. What differentiates us? Our people answer the phone and we provide quality personal service. I truly believe the cure for social ills in Indian Country is economic development and job creation.

As Native American Woman business leaders, we have to utilize the power and influence to help those in need in our native communities and reservations. I am proud to speak on issues that affect native women from procurement challenges to violence against women and children.

Stand up and make a difference . . . but do this on your own terms.

Margo Gray-Proctor

TRIBE: Osage Nation

RECOMMENDED BOOKS: *Smart Women Take Risks* by Helene Lerner, *You're Hired* by Bill Rancic

SOCIAL MEDIA: FACEBOOK: Horizon Engineering Services Co. and Margo Gray-Proctor

TWITTER: ndn_bosslady

LINKEDIN: Horizon Engineering Services Co. and Margo Gray-Proctor

WEBSITE: www.horizonengineeringservicesco.com

EDITOR'S NOTES: Margo Gray-Proctor is a survivor of domestic abuse and a cancer survivor. Margo has served her community, nation and Indian Country. For this, she has earned many titles and awards, although she says her favorite titles are *Mom* and *Grandma.* Margo is President of Horizon Engineering Services consulting with tribes on transportation planning, gaming/casino developments, project management, research for environmental assessment, scheduling, master planning, conceptual, preliminary and final design, bidding and negotiations phase and construction phase of projects. Margo has built a profitable and award winning business in a male dominated industry.

She is the Chairwoman of the National Center for American Indian Enterprise Development—NCAIED, the first native woman to hold this position. Margo has held positions as a Board Member for the National American Indian Chamber of Commerce and an American Indian Business Network Board Member for the National Indian Gaming Association (NIGA). She is a member of the National Congress of American Indians, National Indian Gaming Association, Intertribal Transportation Association, Women Impacting

Public Policy, and Women Empowering Women for Indian Nations.

Margo has won numerous awards and recently was selected as *The Journal Record's 50 Making a Difference* recognizing Oklahoma's leading women. She also received the *Badger Award for Tenacity and Perseverance in Business* by the American Indian Business Leaders Association and the *Georgeann Robinson Humanitarian Award* presented by the Oklahoma Federation of Indian Women. Her flagship company, Horizon Engineering Services Co., was the 2007 recipient of the *State Business of the Year* award bestowed by the American Indian Chamber of Commerce of Oklahoma, the 2005 recipient of the National Center for American Indian Enterprise Development's *Indian Business Owner of the Year* award, and the 2004 recipient of the National Indian Business Association's *Outstanding National Native American Woman-Owned Business* award. Margo has been featured in www.workingwomen.com and *Smart Women Take Risks*, a book by Helene Learner.

Mrs. Gray-Proctor is also an internationally known speaker on Native American Economic Development, Business, Minority and Women's issues.

Margo holds the honor of Head Cook in her Native American church. She is married to Adam Proctor and has three sons and seven grandchildren.

Bibliography

1. Bataille, G. M., & Lisa, L. (Ed.). (2001). *Native American Women: A Biographical Dictionary* (2nd ed.). New York: Routledge.

2. Center for Women's Business Research, 2004.

3. Hosmer, B., & O'Neill C. (Ed.). (2004). *Native Pathways: American Indian Culture and Economic Development in the Twentieth Century.* Boulder: University Press of Colorado.

4. Meyer, C. J., & Royer, D. (Ed.). (2001). *Selling the Indian.* Tuscan: The University of Arizona Press.

5. R. Miller (2008). *American Indian Entrepreneurs: Unique Challenges, Unlimited Potential.* Arizona State Law Journal. Vol. 40, 2008.

6. Sonneborn, L. (1998). *A to Z of Native American Women*. New York: Facts on File, Inc.

Submit Your Story

Are you an entrepreneur with a story to share? Join us in our quest to encourage others by describing your unique journey to becoming an entrepreneur! The series of books, *A Cup of Cappuccino for the Entrepreneur's Spirit,* captures entrepreneurs' true stories, which are written to inspire, energize and teach the reader. The stories include adversities, challenges, triumphs, and successes experienced by the entrepreneur to help readers discover passion and basic principles they can use to live the entrepreneurial dream.

The *Cappuccino* series of books includes *Volumes I, II,* the *Women Entrepreneurs' Edition* and the *American Indian Women Entrepreneurs' Edition.* The *Extraordinary Entrepreneurs' Edition* will be released in 2012. If you are interested in sharing your story to inspire others, the format and guidelines are located on the website at www.acupofcappuccino.com. Just click on Submit Story.

www.ingramcontent.com/pod-product-compliance
Lightning Source LLC
Chambersburg PA
CBHW061603110426
42742CB00039B/2686